CROWN FINANCIAL MINIS

Biblical Financial Study

PRACTICAL APPLICATION WORKBOOK

PO Box 100
Gainesville GA 30503-0100
(800) 722-1976 / www.crown.org

ISBN 1-893946-15-0

September 2000 edition

TABLE OF CONTENTS

Week	Item	Pages
	Workbook Explanation	3
	Personal Information Sheet	5
2	Personal Financial Statement/Recording Income & Spending	7-13
3	Deed/Financial Goals	15-21
4	Debt List/Debt Repayment Schedule	23-30
5	Estimated Budget	31-37
6	Adjusting Your Budget	39-43
7	Beginning Your Budget	45-83
8	Your Checking Account/Budgeting Hints	85-88
9	Organizing Your Estate	89-93
10	Organizing Your Insurance/Filing Systems	95-97
11	Organizing Your Children	99-103
12	Determining Your Standard of Living/Wise Spending Hints	105-107
	Involvement and Suggestions	109-110
	Resources	111
	Memory Verses	

WORKBOOK EXPLANATION

Each week during the study you will be assigned a practical application to complete. This workbook contains an explanation of each week's assignment, a completed sample of each practical application, and blank worksheets for you to finish.

The pages are perforated for easy removal and punched for a three-ring notebook should you desire to place them in such a binder. We suggest you complete the forms in pencil so that you may make changes easily. If you are married, please complete these with your spouse. Students of this study are authorized to make photocopies of the forms for their personal use but for no other purpose.

The CD-ROM located in the back of this workbook contains many helpful items. All the forms in the workbook are in electronic form, and the verses you will memorize are set to music. A debt repayment calculator and much more are also included.

We encourage you to visit CROWN's Web site at **www.crown.org** where you will find more detailed information on many financial subjects and links to other helpful web sites. Material orders can be placed online or by calling **1-800-722-1976**.

We pray that these practical exercises will genuinely help you apply the financial principles of Scripture.

This week there are two practical applications to complete—a Deed and your Financial Goals.

THE DEED

To help recognize God's ownership of our possessions, we will complete an exercise transferring the ownership of our possessions to the Lord. We will use a Deed, because one is often used to transfer the ownership of property. This deed is not a legally binding document. It is solely for your use and will not be collected. By completing this Deed on page 17, we establish a time when we acknowledge God's ownership. The following directions will help you to complete the Deed:

1. Insert today's date at the top of the Deed. Then print your first name in the space after "From," because you are transferring ownership of your possessions to another.

2. There is a large blank space following the sentence: "I (we) hereby transfer to the Lord the ownership of the following possessions." Please pray about those possessions you wish to acknowledge that God owns, and write them in the space.

3. In the lower right-hand corner there are two blank lines under the heading "Stewards." This is the space for your signature. If you are married, both you and your spouse should sign. In the lower left-hand corner there are four blank lines for the signatures of witnesses. Bring the completed Deed to your class this coming week and have the others in your group witness your signature to help hold you accountable to recognize God as owner of your possessions.

FINANCIAL GOALS

Determining your financial goals will help you accomplish what is important to you. Here's how to proceed:

1. Complete the Financial Goals worksheet on pages 20 and 21. If you are married, we recommend that you and your spouse individually write down your financial goals on separate sheets of paper. Then compare goals and compile a complete list on the Financial Goals worksheet.

2. Pray for the Lord to confirm your goals. Do not limit yourself by your present circumstances. Remember the division of financial responsibilities: Our part and God's part. Our part is to do what we can as faithful stewards. God's part is to meet our needs and dispense possessions as He sees fit. Many of your goals may be "faith goals" that you must trust the Lord to provide. Then prioritize your goals. For instance, funding education might be more important than buying a boat. Also, you don't have to accomplish all your goals at once. For example, your budget may not allow you to save as much as you want for retirement until your children are educated.

3. List your goals for the coming year. One caution: Do not set unrealistic goals. It's better to accomplish three goals than to become frustrated with ten unattainable ones.

Quit Claim Deed

This Quit Claim Deed, Made the __15th__ day of __May__

From: **Don and Janet**

To: The Lord

I (we) hereby transfer to the Lord the ownership of the following possessions:

Home	Golf clubs
Don's car	Sewing machine
Janet's car	Stamp collection
Clothes	Don's job
Savings account	Wedding rings
Boat	Children's educational fund
Furniture	Antique piano
Rental property	IBM stock
Retirement account	Pension fund
TV	

Witnesses who hold me (us) accountable
in the recognition of the Lord's ownership:

Ima Watchin

Nosit All

Ura Countable

Bea Faithful

Stewards of the possessions above:

Don

Janet

This instrument is not a binding legal document and cannot be used to transfer property.

Quit Claim Deed

This Quit Claim Deed, Made the _____ day of _____

From: _____

To: The Lord

I (we) hereby transfer to the Lord the ownership of the following possessions:

Witnesses who hold me (us) accountable
in the recognition of the Lord's ownership:

Stewards of the possessions above:

_____

_____

_____

_____

_____

_____

This instrument is not a binding legal document and cannot be used to transfer property.

Financial Goals

Date: January 1

GIVING GOALS:

Would like to give **15** percent of my income.

Other giving goals: Contribute $5,000 to world missions over the next ten years and help support one needy child

DEBT REPAYMENT GOALS:

Would like to pay off the following debts first:

Creditor	Amount
Sears	100.00
Visa	900.00
Crazy Eddie's Auto Sales	4,000.00
Last National Bank	2,000.00

EDUCATIONAL GOALS:

Would like to fund the following education:

Person	School	Annual Cost	Total Cost
John	Vo-Tech	4,000.00	12,000.00
Ruth	State College	8,000.00	32,000.00

Other educational goals: Janet would like to study to become a registered nurse

LIFESTYLE GOALS:

Would like to make the following major purchases: (home, automobile, travel, etc.)

Item	Amount
Add Porch to Home	8,000.00
Replace Janet's Car	7,500.00
Replace Refrigerator	800.00

Would like to achieve the following annual income: **$52,000.00**

FINANCIAL GOALS

SAVINGS AND INVESTMENT GOALS:

Would like to save __10__ percent on my income.

Other savings goals: __Increase savings to 15 percent a year within ten years__

Would like to make the following investments: Investment

Rental property	15,000.00 down payment
Retirement account	2,000.00 each year
Mutual fund	2,000.00 each year

Would like to provide my/our heirs with the following: __House and rental property__ __paid for and enough insurance to provide an adequate income to meet their needs__

STARTING A BUSINESS:

Would like to invest in or begin my/our own business: __No__

Goals For This Year

I believe the Lord wants me/us to achieve the following goals this year:

Priority	Financial Goals	Our Part	God's Part
1	Increase Giving	Write Check	Provide Money
2	Balance Budget	Reduce Spending	Give Wisdom
3	Pay Off Boat	Sell Boat	Provide Buyer
4			
5			

FINANCIAL GOALS

Financial Goals

Date: _____

GIVING GOALS:

Would like to give _____ percent of my income.

Other giving goals: _____

_____

DEBT REPAYMENT GOALS:

Would like to pay off the following debts first:

Creditor	Amount
_____	_____
_____	_____
_____	_____
_____	_____

EDUCATIONAL GOALS:

Would like to fund the following education:

Person	School	Annual Cost	Total Cost
_____	_____	_____	_____
_____	_____	_____	_____
_____	_____	_____	_____
_____	_____	_____	_____

Other educational goals: _____

_____

LIFESTYLE GOALS:

Would like to make the following major purchases: (home, automobile, travel, etc.)

Item	Amount
_____	_____
_____	_____
_____	_____

Would like to achieve the following annual income: _____

SAVINGS AND INVESTMENT GOALS:

Would like to save _____ percent on my income.

Other savings goals: _____

_____

Would like to make the following investments: Investment

_____   _____

_____   _____

_____   _____

_____   _____

Would like to provide my/our heirs with the following: _____

_____

STARTING A BUSINESS:

Would like to invest in or begin my/our own business: _____

_____

_____

Goals For This Year

I believe the Lord wants me/us to achieve the following goals this year:

Priority	Financial Goals	Our Part	God's Part
1	_____	_____	_____
2	_____	_____	_____
3	_____	_____	_____
4	_____	_____	_____
5	_____	_____	_____

DEBT LIST & REPAYMENT SCHEDULE

This week there are two practical applications to complete: the Debt List and Debt Repayment Schedule.

DEBT LIST

Many people don't know precisely what they owe. The Debt List will assist you in compiling your debts and the terms of each debt. The seven columns on the Debt List are as follows:

1. **Creditor**—The one to whom the debt is owed.

2. **Describe what was purchased**—Item purchased with the money borrowed.

3. **Monthly payment**—The amount of the monthly payment. If payment is due more often than monthly, compute the total amount that is paid each month. For example, a $200 loan payment paid twice each month equals $400 per month. If payment is due less frequently than monthly, determine the average monthly cost. For example, a $600 payment paid twice a year would average $100 each month.

4. **Balance due**—The amount of the outstanding debt.

5. **Scheduled pay-off date**—The date by which the debt will be fully paid.

6. **Interest rate**—The rate of interest charged for the debt.

7. **Payments past due**—The number of payments, if any, past due on each debt.

After entering each debt, add and total the Monthly Payment and the Balance Due columns.

DEBT REPAYMENT SCHEDULE

The next step is to complete a Debt Repayment Schedule for each debt. This will help you be systematic in your effort to get out of debt. There are four blank Debt Repayment Schedules in this workbook. Should you need more, you may photocopy this form. Enter the following information at the top of each Debt Repayment Schedule: the creditor's name, why the money was borrowed, the total amount still owed, the interest rate charged for the loan and today's date. The Debt Repayment Schedule has four columns:

1. **Date due**—The day each payment is due.

2. **Payment amount**—The amount of each payment.

3. **Payments remaining**—The number of payments remaining.

4. **Balance due**—The loan balance due after each payment.

For access to automated debt repayment computations, use the CD-ROM in the back of this workbook.

Debt List

Date: __January 1__

Creditor	Describe What Was Purchased	Monthly Payments	Balance Due	Scheduled Pay Off Date	Interest Rate	Payments Past Due
Sears	Miscellaneous	20.00	100.00	7/2000	18%	0
VISA	Miscellaneous	14.00	900.00	2/2014	15%	1
Last National Bank	Boat	100.00	2,000.00	12/2002	18%	0
Life Insurance	Investment	20.00	3,000.00	None	7%	0
Totals		154.00	6,000.00			

Auto Loans						
Crazy Eddie's Auto Sales		100.00	4,000.00	11/2004	10%	0
Total Auto Loans		100.00	4,000.00			

Home Mortgages						
Second Nat'l Bank	First Mortgage	780.00	75,000.00	1/2021	9%	0
Total Home Mortgages		780.00	75,000.00			

Business/Investment Debt						
Total Business/Investment Debt						

DEBT LIST

Debt List

Date: _____

Creditor	Describe What Was Purchased	Monthly Payments	Balance Due	Scheduled Pay Off Date	Interest Rate	Payments Past Due
Totals						

Auto Loans						
Total Auto Loans						

Home Mortgages						
Total Home Mortgages						

Business/Investment Debt						
Total Business/Investment Debt						

Debt Repayment Schedule

Creditor: __Last National Bank__   Date: __January 1__

Describe What Was Purchased: __Boat__

Amount Owed: __$2,000.00__   Interest Rate: __18%__

Date Due:	Amount	Payments Remaining	Balance Due
Jan. 10	100.00	23	1,930.00
Feb. 10	100.00	22	1,858.95
Mar. 10	100.00	21	1,786.83
Apr. 10	100.00	20	1,713.63
May 10	100.00	19	1,630.33
June 10	100.00	18	1,563.92
July 10	100.00	17	1,487.38
Aug. 10	100.00	16	1,409.69
Sep. 10	100.00	15	1,330.84
Oct. 10	100.00	14	1,250.80
Nov. 10	100.00	13	1,169.56
Dec. 10	100.00	12	1,087.10
Jan. 10	100.00	11	1,003.41
Feb. 10	100.00	10	918.46
Mar. 10	100.00	9	832.20
Apr. 10	100.00	8	744.72
May 10	100.00	7	655.89
June 10	100.00	6	565.73
July 10	100.00	5	474.22
Aug. 10	100.00	4	381.33
Sep. 10	100.00	3	287.05
Oct. 10	100.00	2	191.36
Nov. 10	100.00	1	94.23
Dec. 10	98.54	0	0

Debt Repayment Schedule

Creditor: _____   Date: _____

Describe What Was Purchased: _____

Amount Owed: _____   Interest Rate: _____

Date Due:	Amount	Payments Remaining	Balance Due

Debt Repayment Schedule

Creditor: _____   Date: _____

Describe What Was Purchased: _____

Amount Owed: _____   Interest Rate: _____

Date Due:	Amount	Payments Remaining	Balance Due

Debt Repayment Schedule

Creditor: _____   Date: _____

Describe What Was Purchased: _____

Amount Owed: _____   Interest Rate: _____

Date Due:	Amount	Payments Remaining	Balance Due

Debt Repayment Schedule

Creditor: _____ Date: _____

Describe What Was Purchased: _____

Amount Owed: _____ Interest Rate: _____

Date Due:	Amount	Payments Remaining	Balance Due

A budget is planned spending. A budget is telling your money where you want it to go rather than wondering where it went.

If you are already using a budget that you like, we still want you to complete the practical applications for the CROWN budget because you may learn some techniques that will improve your current budget. It will also be important for you to understand the CROWN system if you lead the study in the future. We heartily recommend the excellent *Money Matters* budgeting software, which is compatible with this budget. This may be ordered by visiting our Web site.

The next step in creating your budget is to complete the Estimated Budget on page 37. This will give you a picture of your current income and spending.

The Estimated Budget is one of the most important practical applications of the entire study, and for many it proves to be difficult. You may not know what you are spending. You may be frustrated and discouraged by what your Estimated Budget reveals.

But take heart—there is hope. You are not alone. Every week for the rest of the study you will be refining a workable budget. Complete the following steps.

DETERMINE MONTHLY INCOME

1. LIST MONTHLY GROSS INCOME

List all income (income before deductions) in the "Gross Monthly Income" section on page 37. Under "Other Income", include any of the following that you may receive:

Commissions	_____
Bonuses	_____
Tips	_____
Retirement income	_____
Net business income	_____
Net rents	_____
Total Other Income	

When all or part of your income consists of commissions or other fluctuating sources, estimate it for a year and divide by twelve to compute your average monthly income.

Business expense reimbursements should not be considered income. Avoid the temptation to spend expense money as if it were income. This can lead to increased debt when those bills come due.

2. SUBTRACT GIVING AND TAXES

The next step is to determine the amount you give and your taxes. This is the portion of your gross income that cannot be spent for living expenses.

☑ CATEGORY 1—Tithe/Giving

Include all that you give to:

The church	_____
The poor	_____
Other ministries	_____
Other giving	_____
Total Tithe/Giving	☐

☑ CATEGORY 2—Taxes

Deduct federal withholdings, social security, and state and local taxes from gross income. Self-employed individuals must regularly set aside money for taxes. Beware of the tendency to treat unpaid tax money as money you can spend.

   Other Deductions: Payroll deductions for insurance, savings, debt payments, investments, retirement, union dues, etc. should not be subtracted from gross income. Include them in spendable income and deduct them from the proper category so that you will have a more accurate picture of your spending. For example, if a payroll deduction is made for health insurance, this amount should be considered as a part of your gross income and then noted as an expense under the Insurance Category.

3. COMPUTE NET SPENDABLE INCOME

Subtract Category 1 (Tithe/Giving) and Category 2 (Taxes) from the Gross Monthly Income to determine the Net Spendable Income.

HOW IS NET SPENDABLE INCOME BEING SPENT— WHAT ARE MY LIVING EXPENSES?

Living Expenses are divided into twelve categories (Category 3 through Category 14). Each category is described more fully, as follows:

☑ CATEGORY 3—Housing

All monthly expenses necessary to operate the home, including mortgage or rent payments, taxes, insurance, maintenance, utilities, telephone, and any furnishings you plan to purchase or improvements you anticipate making. The amount used for utility payments should be an average monthly amount for the past twelve months.

   If you cannot establish an accurate maintenance expense, use 10% of the monthly mortgage payment.

☑ CATEGORY 4—Food

All grocery expenses, including paper goods and non-food products normally purchased at grocery or convenience stores.

☑ CATEGORY 5—Transportation

Include automobile payments, insurance, gas, oil, maintenance, tolls, parking, licenses, taxes, repair and replacement, and mass transit fares.

ESTIMATED BUDGET

The amount of money you set aside for repair and replacement should be sufficient to keep the car in decent repair and to replace it periodically. If replacement funds currently are not available in the budget, the minimum allocation should be maintenance costs. Annual or semi-annual automobile insurance payments should be set aside on a monthly basis to avoid the crisis of a neglected expense.

CATEGORY 6 — Insurance

Include all insurance, such as health, life, and disability, except those associated with the home or automobile.

CATEGORY 7 — Debts

Include all monthly payments required to meet debt obligations. Home mortgage and automobile payments are not included here. Refer to the Debt List on page 25.

CATEGORY 8 — Entertainment and Recreation

Include vacations, camping trips, club dues, sporting equipment, hobby expenses, sporting events, books, videos, and pets. Include eating out and daily lunches eaten away from home.

CATEGORY 9 — Clothing

Estimate the average annual amount spent on clothing divided by 12. This category is often underestimated.

CATEGORY 10 — Savings

Allocate something for savings. A savings account can provide funds for emergencies and is crucial to good planning.

CATEGORY 11 — Medical

Include health insurance deductible, medical bills, eye glasses, prescriptions, dentist, etc. Use a yearly average divided by 12 to determine the monthly amount.

CATEGORY 12 — Miscellaneous

Expenses that do not fit anywhere else are included in the miscellaneous category.

CATEGORY 13 — Investments

Individuals and families with surplus income in their budgets will have the opportunity to invest to meet their long-term financial goals. As you begin to budget regularly, hopefully more money will be freed to be allocated to this category.

CATEGORY 14 — School/Child Care

School tuition, tutoring, school books and materials, music/dance lessons, day care, and any other similar expenses are included in this category.

DETERMINING THE SURPLUS OR DEFICIT

STEP ONE: In the lower right-hand corner of page 37 insert the Net Spendable Income. Then add the expenses under each of the Categories 3 through 14 and note this on the Total Living Expenses line. Subtract Total Living Expenses from Net Spendable Income to determine whether you have a surplus or deficit in your budget.

STEP TWO: *If income is greater than expenses,* you have a **surplus** and need only to control spending to maximize the surplus. Using a budget will help you accomplish this.

STEP THREE: *If expenses are greater than income,* you have a **deficit** and a careful review will be necessary to bring the budget into balance. You will begin to work on this next week.

COMPUTING THE VARIABLE EXPENSES

To establish an accurate Estimated Budget, you need to be able to budget spending that varies each month. These include:

- **Irregular monthly expenses**—such as utility bills and food. Compute the average monthly cost by determining the total annual amount spent for an item and divide by 12.

- **Expenses that do not occur every month**—such as auto maintenance, medical expenses, clothing, vacations, etc.

Examine the table below to see how to determine average monthly spending that does not occur each month. For example, if you spend $600 a year for automobile insurance that is paid quarterly, set aside $50 per month so that the bill can be paid when due. Use the blank table on page 35 to compute your variable expenses.

	Estimated Yearly Cost	÷ 12 =	Estimated Cost Per Month
1. Vacation	720		60
2. Dentist	120		10
3. Doctor	240		20
4. Automobile			
5. Life Insurance			
6. Health Insurance			
7. Auto Insurance	600		50
8. Home Insurance			
9. Clothing	1,128		94
10. Investments			
11. Other			

	Estimated Yearly Cost	÷ 12 =	Estimated Cost Per Month
1. Vacation	_____		_____
2. Dentist	_____		_____
3. Doctor	_____		_____
4. Automobile	_____		_____
5. Life Insurance	_____		_____
6. Health Insurance	_____		_____
7. Auto Insurance	_____		_____
8. Home Insurance	_____		_____
9. Clothing	_____		_____
10. Investments	_____		_____
11. Other	_____		_____
	_____		_____

WHAT IF MY INCOME IS NOT PREDICTABLE?

Some people reason that they cannot keep a budget because they do not receive steady, predictable income. However, that is all the more reason why it is important for them to budget! If your income is not consistent, such as that of a self-employed person or a commission salesperson, make a conservative estimate of what you anticipate as your yearly income and divide by 12 to determine your average monthly income.

It is important for those whose income is unpredictable to work toward establishing a savings reserve from which they can draw a steady income. For example, assume a family is able to save $5,000 for this savings reserve and their budget is $3,000 a month. If they earn $2,000 during the month, they would withdraw $1,000 from the savings to balance their budget. If they earn $5,000 the next month, they would spend only the $3,000 they have budgeted and deposit $2,000 into the savings reserve. The biggest challenge for those with unpredictable income is to save the reserve and not spend everything they earn during a high income month.

ESTIMATED BUDGET

MONTHLY INCOME

GROSS MONTHLY INCOME | 4,040

Salary — 4,000
Interest — 5
Dividends — 15
Other Income — 20

LESS

1. Tithe/Giving | 250
2. Taxes (Fed., State, FICA) | 835

NET SPENDABLE INCOME | 2,955

MONTHLY LIVING EXPENSES

3. Housing | 1101

Mortgage/Rent — 780
Insurance — 28
Property Taxes — 68
Electricity — 85
Gas — 16
Water — 10
Sanitation — 0
Telephone — 25
Maintenance — 68
Cable TV — 21
Other — 0

4. Food | 338

5. Transportation | 368

Payments — 100
Gas & Oil — 80
Insurance — 50
License/Taxes — 38
Maint./Repair/Replace — 100
Other — 0

6. Insurance | 83

Life — 30
Health — 53
Other — 0

7. Debts | 154

(Except auto & house payment; see page 25.)

8. Entertainment/Recreation | 242

Eating Out — 127
Baby-sitters — 0
Activities/Trips — 20
Vacation — 60
Pets — 35
Other — 0

9. Clothing | 94

10. Savings | 165

11. Medical Expenses | 40

Doctor — 20
Dentist — 10
Prescriptions — 10
Other — 0

12. Miscellaneous | 281

Toiletries/Cosmetics — 19
Beauty/Barber — 41
Laundry/Cleaning — 35
Allowances — 66
Subscriptions — 20
Gifts (incl. Christmas) — 50
Cash — 50
Other — 0

13. Investments | 0

14. School/Child Care

Tuition — 200
Materials — 16
Transportation — 0
Day Care — 0 | 216

TOTAL LIVING EXPENSES | 3,082

INCOME VS. LIVING EXPENSES

NET SPENDABLE INCOME | 2,955

LESS TOTAL LIVING EXPENSES | 3,082

SURPLUS OR DEFICIT | -127

ESTIMATED BUDGET

Estimated Budget

MONTHLY INCOME

GROSS MONTHLY INCOME ☐

Salary _____
Interest _____
Dividends _____
Other Income _____

LESS

1. Tithe/Giving ☐
2. Taxes (Fed., State, FICA) ☐

NET SPENDABLE INCOME ☐

MONTHLY LIVING EXPENSES

3. Housing ☐
   Mortgage/Rent _____
   Insurance _____
   Property Taxes _____
   Electricity _____
   Gas _____
   Water _____
   Sanitation _____
   Telephone _____
   Maintenance _____
   Cable TV _____
   Other _____

4. Food ☐

5. Transportation ☐
   Payments _____
   Gas & Oil _____
   Insurance _____
   License/Taxes _____
   Maint./Repair/Replace _____
   Other _____

6. Insurance ☐
   Life _____
   Health _____
   Other _____

7. Debts ☐

(Except auto & house payment; see page 25.)

8. Entertainment/Recreation ☐
   Eating Out _____
   Baby-sitters _____
   Activities/Trips _____
   Vacation _____
   Pets _____
   Other _____

9. Clothing ☐

10. Savings ☐

11. Medical Expenses ☐
    Doctor _____
    Dentist _____
    Prescriptions _____
    Other _____

12. Miscellaneous ☐
    Toiletries/Cosmetics _____
    Beauty/Barber _____
    Laundry/Cleaning _____
    Allowances _____
    Subscriptions _____
    Gifts (incl. Christmas) _____
    Cash _____
    Other _____

13. Investments ☐

14. School/Child Care ☐
    Tuition _____
    Materials _____
    Transportation _____
    Day Care _____

TOTAL LIVING EXPENSES ☐

INCOME VS. LIVING EXPENSES

NET SPENDABLE INCOME ☐

LESS TOTAL LIVING EXPENSES ☐

SURPLUS OR DEFICIT ☐

ESTIMATED BUDGET

Last week when you completed your Estimated Budget and subtracted your spending from your income, did you have more income than spending? For many people the answer is no! They discover that current spending adds up to more than their income.

Your assignment this week is to adjust and balance your budget. The best way to do this is to review each income and spending category. Can you think of any ideas to increase your income? Then ask yourself these two questions about each spending category: Do I really need this? Can I purchase this less expensively?

Some of the decisions will be difficult to make. It is not easy to reduce spending. It may be necessary to consider a change in housing, automobiles, insurance, or private schools. But the freedom of balancing your budget, getting out of debt, giving more generously, and funding your financial goals is worth the sacrifice.

AMOUNT NEEDED TO BALANCE YOUR BUDGET

If your Estimated Budget shows that you are spending more than your income, the last line which is titled "Surplus or Deficit" will be a negative number. Study Don and Janet's example on page 36. In their case there was a deficit of $127 a month in their Estimated Budget. To balance their budget, they made the following decisions:

Janet began working out of the home 10 hours a week as a bookkeeper earning $400 a month.

Their taxes increased $65 a month.

They increased their giving to 10 percent of their gross income.

They stopped using cable TV and saved $21 a month.

Don starting carpooling which saved $40 a month in transportation.

They increased their saving to $200 a month.

They began investing $40 a month.

Turn to page 44 to examine their balanced Estimated Budget.

As you think of ways to increase your income or reduce spending, adjust the appropriate item on your Estimated Budget on page 37. Continue adjusting until your budget is balanced or you have a surplus. Remember to do this in pencil.

As you begin balancing your budget, it may be helpful to compare the percentage of your income that you spend in each category with that of the average balanced budget.

1. PERCENTAGE GUIDE

The purpose of the Percentage Guide on page 41 is to indicate problem areas. *The percentages are not absolutes!* Actual percentages vary because different factors will influence what you spend, such as the cost of housing in your area and the number of children you might have.

The Guide is a standard against which you can compare present spending patterns. It will enable you to identify potential areas of overspending that need to be adjusted. The percentages are based on a family of four with incomes ranging from $25,000 to $125,000 per year. Above or below these limits, the percentages may change according to your situation and needs. In the lower income levels, basic needs will dominate income distribution.

2. PERCENTAGE BUDGET

The Percentage Budget will help you compute what you should be spending based on the Percentage Guide.

Examine Don and Janet's Percentage Budget on page 42. They entered their annual income at the top of the page and their Gross Monthly Income on the next line. They subtracted their Tithe/Giving and Taxes from the Gross Monthly Income to determine Net Spendable Income. From the Percentage Guide on page 41, they took the percentages from the column ($45,000) closest to their annual income of $48,000, and entered them on the Percentage Budget. For example, their housing is 32%. Complete the Percentage Budget on page 44 based on your income or use the CD-ROM or visit our Web site to compute this electronically.

(Reminder: If you have School/Child Care expenses, the percentage for this category must be deducted from other budget categories. In Don and Janet's example, they reduced the Investment category from 7% to 2%.)

3. COMPARE

Now, compare your Estimated Budget on page 37 with your Percentage Budget on page 43. It is not necessary that your balanced budget fit in the Percentage Budget. It is necessary that your spending not exceed your income!!!

After you identify the categories where there is overspending, decisions must be made. It may be possible to reduce some areas to compensate for overspending in others. For example, if housing expenditures are high, it may be necessary to reduce spending in other areas such as entertainment and transportation.

ADJUSTING YOUR BUDGET

Percentage Guide

Gross Income	25,000	35,000	45,000	55,000	85,000	125,000
1. Tithe/Giving	2,500	3,500	4,500	5,500	8,500	12,500
2. Taxes[1]	3,250	6,650	9,000	11,550	18,000	30,000
Net Spendable	**19,250**	**24,850**	**31,500**	**37,950**	**58,500**	**82,500**
3. Housing	38%	36%	32%	30%	30%	30%
4. Food	14%	12%	12%	12%	11%	11%
5. Transportation	14%	12%	13%	13%	13%	12%
6. Insurance	5%	5%	5%	5%	5%	5%
7. Debts	5%	5%	5%	5%	5%	5%
8. Entertainment/ Recreation	4%	6%	7%	7%	7%	8%
9. Clothing	5%	5%	5%	6%	7%	7%
10. Savings	5%	5%	5%	5%	5%	5%
11. Medical / Dental	5%	4%	4%	4%	4%	4%
12. Miscellaneous	5%	5%	5%	5%	5%	5%
13. Investments[2]	0%	5%	7%	8%	8%	8%
If you have school/child care expenses, these percentages must be deducted from other categories.						
14. School/Child Care	8%	6%	5%	5%	5%	5%

1. The tax category includes taxes for Social Security and a small amount for state taxes. To be completely accurate, you will need to calculate your actual taxes. The tax code changes regularly. Please be sure to insert your actual tax into this category.
2. This category is used to fund long-term goals such as college education or retirement.

Percentage Budget

ANNUAL INCOME: $ __48,000__

Gross Monthly Income	4,040
1. Tithe/Giving	250
2. Tax	835
Net Spendable Income	2,955

SPENDING CATEGORY	PERCENTAGE	NET SPENDABLE INCOME			AMOUNT
3. Housing	32%	x	2,955	=	945
4. Food	12%	x	2,955	=	355
5. Transportation	13%	x	2,955	=	384
6. Insurance	5%	x	2,955	=	148
7. Debts	5%	x	2,955	=	148
8. Entertainment/Recreation	7%	x	2,955	=	207
9. Clothing	5%	x	2,955	=	148
10. Savings	5%	x	2,955	=	148
11. Medical/Dental	4%	x	2,955	=	117
12. Miscellaneous	5%	x	2,955	=	148
13. Investments	2%	x	2,955	=	59
14. School/Child Care[1]	5%	x	2,955	=	148
TOTAL: (cannot exceed Net Spendable Income)					2,955

[1] If you have this expense, this percentage must be deducted from other budget categories.

Percentage Budget

ANNUAL INCOME:	$ _____	

Gross Monthly Income ☐

  1. Tithe/Giving ☐

  2. Tax ☐

Net Spendable Income ☐

SPENDING CATEGORY	PERCENTAGE	NET SPENDABLE INCOME	AMOUNT
3. Housing	_____ x	_____ =	☐
4. Food	_____ x	_____ =	☐
5. Transportation	_____ x	_____ =	☐
6. Insurance	_____ x	_____ =	☐
7. Debts	_____ x	_____ =	☐
8. Entertainment/Recreation	_____ x	_____ =	☐
9. Clothing	_____ x	_____ =	☐
10. Savings	_____ x	_____ =	☐
11. Medical/Dental	_____ x	_____ =	☐
12. Miscellaneous	_____ x	_____ =	☐
13. Investments	_____ x	_____ =	☐
14. School/Child Care[1]	_____ x	_____ =	☐
TOTAL: (cannot exceed Net Spendable Income)			☐

[1] If you have this expense, this percentage must be deducted from other budget categories.

Estimated Budget

MONTHLY INCOME

GROSS MONTHLY INCOME | 4,440
Salary | 4,400
Interest | 5
Dividends | 15
Other Income | 20

LESS

1. Tithe/Giving | 444
2. Taxes (Fed., State, FICA) | 900

NET SPENDABLE INCOME | 3,096

MONTHLY LIVING EXPENSES

3. Housing | 1,080
   Mortgage/Rent | 780
   Insurance | 28
   Property Taxes | 68
   Electricity | 85
   Gas | 16
   Water | 10
   Sanitation | 0
   Telephone | 25
   Maintenance | 68
   Cable TV | 0
   Other | 0

4. Food | 338

5. Transportation | 328
   Payments | 100
   Gas & Oil | 40
   Insurance | 50
   License/Taxes | 38
   Maint./Repair/Replace | 100
   Other | 0

6. Insurance | 83
   Life | 30
   Health | 53
   Other | 0

7. Debts | 154

(Except auto & house payment; see page 25.)

8. Entertainment/Recreation | 242
   Eating Out | 127
   Baby-sitters | 0
   Activities/Trips | 20
   Vacation | 60
   Pets | 35
   Other | 0

9. Clothing | 94

10. Savings | 200

11. Medical Expenses | 40
    Doctor | 20
    Dentist | 10
    Prescriptions | 10
    Other | 0

12. Miscellaneous | 281
    Toiletries/Cosmetics | 19
    Beauty/Barber | 41
    Laundry/Cleaning | 35
    Allowances | 66
    Subscriptions | 20
    Gifts (incl. Christmas) | 50
    Cash | 50
    Other | 0

13. Investments | 40

14. School/Child Care | 216
    Tuition | 200
    Materials | 16
    Transportation | 0
    Day Care | 0

TOTAL LIVING EXPENSES | 3,096

INCOME VS. LIVING EXPENSES

NET SPENDABLE INCOME | 3,096

LESS TOTAL LIVING EXPENSES | 3,096

SURPLUS OR DEFICIT | 0

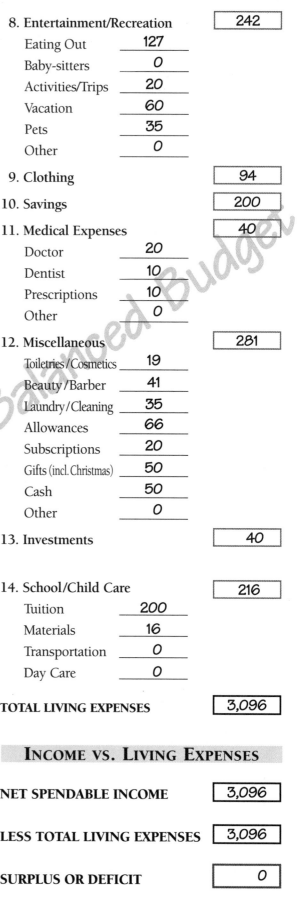

ESTIMATED BUDGET

This week you will set up and begin your budget. The most common reason a budget is not used is because it's too complicated. With that in mind, we designed a budget that is simple to use.

BEGINNING YOUR BUDGET

ENTER BUDGETED AMOUNT

First, go to your balanced Estimated Budget on page 37. From the Estimated Budget enter the amounts you have budgeted for income and each of the fourteen spending categories on the first line of the Monthly Budget sheet on pages 52 and 53. The line is titled "Budgeted Amount."

Examine Don and Janet's sample. They took the figures from their balanced Estimated Budget on page 44 and recorded their budgeted income of $4,440, their Tithe/Giving of $444, and so forth on their Monthly Budget on pages 50 and 51.

INCOME

Every time you receive income, enter the amount you receive on the Income column. Don received his paycheck on the first day of the month. His gross pay was $2,000, and he had $450 taken out for taxes.

SPENDING

Every time you spend, record the amount in the proper category. Don and Janet gave $200 to their church on the first day of the month.

CHECK YOUR PROGRESS

Anytime during the month you can determine how well you are doing with your budget simply by adding all you have spent in a particular category and comparing it to your budgeted amount. For example, if you want to buy a shirt but are not sure you have enough left, add up what you have spent for clothes and compare the total with your clothing budget.

We recommend that you do this for every category mid-way through the month on the line titled "Subtotal This Month" to help you monitor your budget.

Spending can be done in a variety of ways, such as check, cash, credit cards, debit cards or electronic transfer. The CROWN budget is designed to allow you to account for all of these different methods of spending as simply as possible.

SPENDING BY CHECK

Each time you write a check, immediately record it in your checking account register, then enter it on the Monthly Budget sheet. Examine Don and Janet's checkbook register below. They recorded their donation of $200 to First Church by check #101 in their checking account register, then entered $200 on their Monthly Budget under Tithe/Giving.

DATE	CHECK NUMBER	CHECKS ISSUED TO OR DEPOSIT RECEIVED FROM	AMOUNT OF DEPOSIT	✓	AMOUNT OF CHECK	BALANCE
1/1	DEP.	Don's Salary	2,000.00	✓		2,000.00
1/1	101	First Church			200.00	1,800.00
1/1	102	Savings			100.00	1,700.00
1/3	103	Good Gas Station			35.00	1,665.00

Month **February**   Year

Monthly Budget

category	INCOME	TITHE/GIVING	TAXES	HOUSING	FOOD
BUDGETED AMOUNT	$ 4,440	$ 444	$ 900	$ 1,080	$ 338
Date					
1	2,000	200	450		
2					

If you have an electronic withdrawal from your checking account, record it in the same way as a check. Enter it on your checking account register and subtract it from your balance. Then record it on the Monthly Budget sheet.

SPENDING BY CASH

When you spend cash, keep a note of the amount and category or obtain a receipt and write the category on it. Later record the amount spent under the proper category on the Monthly Budget sheet.

SPENDING BY CREDIT CARD

When you use a credit card, retain the receipt to record the transaction under the appropriate Category on the Monthly Budget sheet. If you promptly record your credit card expenditures on the Monthly Budget sheet, you will have enough in your checking account to pay the credit card statement when you receive it and avoid costly finance charges.

When you write the check to pay for your credit card charges, you need not record this on the Monthly Budget sheet as you have already entered the transactions.

1. CURRENT MONTH

INCOME

At the end of the month, add all the income that you have received and record the total on the "This Month Total" line. Now compare the total income with the budgeted income. If you received less than the budgeted income, enter the difference as a negative number on the "This Month Surplus/Deficit" line. If you received more income than you budgeted, this number will be positive.

Examine Don and Janet's Monthly Budget on pages 50 and 51. They received income of $4,550, which was $110 more than their budgeted income of $4,440.

SPENDING

At the end of the month, add all that you have spent in each of the fourteen spending categories and record the totals on the "This Month Total" line. Then subtract each total from the budgeted amount of the category to determine whether you have a surplus or a deficit. Don and Janet budgeted $1,080 for their housing, but spent $1,100, therefore they had a deficit of $20.

2. YEAR TO DATE

INCOME

To determine how well you are doing in each category for the year, simply add this month's "Budgeted Amount" to the previous month's "Year to Date Budget" to determine the current "Year to Date Budget." Then add this month's "Total Income" to last month's "Year to Date Total" to find the current "Year to Date Total Income." Subtract the "Year to Date Total" from the "Year to Date Budget" to determine whether you have a surplus or deficit.

SPENDING

Don and Janet added February's "Budgeted Amount" income of $4,440 with their previous month's "Year to Date Budget" income of $4,440 for a total of $8,880. Then they added February's "Year to Date Total" income of $4,550 with last month's $4,040 "Year to Date Total" which added up to $8,590. Then they subtracted the $8,590 "Year to Date Total" from the $8,880 "Year to Date Budget" and discovered that they have received $290 less income so far this year than budgeted.

Do the same with each of the 14 spending categories.

To find out how you are doing with your entire budget, look at the three boxes at the bottom of the Monthly Budget.

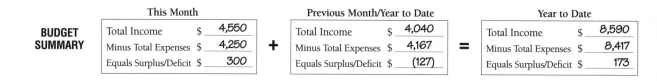

BUDGET SUMMARY

This Month

Total Income	$	4,550
Minus Total Expenses	$	4,250
Equals Surplus/Deficit	$	300

+

Previous Month/Year to Date

Total Income	$	4,040
Minus Total Expenses	$	4,167
Equals Surplus/Deficit	$	(127)

=

Year to Date

Total Income	$	8,590
Minus Total Expenses	$	8,417
Equals Surplus/Deficit	$	173

THIS MONTH

To discover how you did for this month, in the left-hand box titled This Month enter: "This Month Total" income and "This Month Total" spending from all 14 spending categories. Then subtract your spending from your income to determine if you spent more or less than your income. Look at Don and Janet's example above. Their total income this month was $4,550 and they spent a total of $4,250 for a surplus of $300 for the month.

YEAR TO DATE

To find how you are doing for the year, enter in the middle box titled "Previous Month/Year to Date," the figures from last month's "Year to Date" box. Then add the figures from the "This Month" box to the "Previous Month/Year to Date" box to arrive at the totals for the "Year to Date" box. Don and Janet have a surplus of $173 so far this year.

A SURPLUS

If you have a surplus at the end of the month, do not think that you automatically have extra money to spend. You will need to have a surplus at the end of several months to meet some expenses (automobile insurance, real estate taxes, and the like) that are annual or semi-annual expenses. Enter these in full as they occur. These categories will even out over time.

REVIEW YOUR BUDGET

Budgeting is a journey. Do not become discouraged if you do not have a surplus when you first begin. Remember your budget is your friend because it will help you achieve the financial goals that are important to you.

When you finish your budget at the end of each month, review your income and spending to decide whether you should adjust your budget. For example, you may discover that you regularly receive more income than you have budgeted. Or you may find that you usually spend more in a spending category than you have budgeted. Simply alter your budget accordingly.

We pray that you will establish the long-term habit of budgeting to enjoy financial stability and reach your God-given financial goals.

BEGINNING YOUR BUDGET

The Category Page may be used for detailed information on a particular spending category. Using the Category Page will enable you to more accurately analyze your spending.

Don and Janet decided to use the Category Page for Housing and Transportation because they overspend in both categories. Examine their Category Page for Housing.

Category Page
(Individual Account Page)

HOUSING
SPENDING CATEGORY

DATE	CK. #	TRANSACTION	DEPOSIT		WITHDRAWAL		BALANCE	
2/1		Budgeted Amount	1,080	00			1,080	00
2/2	Cash	Plant Store			36	00	1044	00
2/5	105	Second National Bank			780	00	264	00
2/13	108	City Gas Co.			17	00	247	00
2/18	110	Best Paint Store			21	00	226	00
2/19	111	Bell Telephone			26	00	200	00
2/24	113	Reliable Plumbing			85	00	115	00
2/24	114	Fidelity Insurance			28	00	87	00
2/27	116	Edison Electric			97	00	(10	00)
2/27	117	Pure Water Co.			10	00	(20	00)

Don and Janet discovered they will need to make adjustments in their spending for Housing. They spent $20 more in February than they had budgeted. And although they budgeted $68 a month for annual property taxes, they were not able to set aside any money for this future expense.

BEGINNING YOUR BUDGET

Monthly Budget

Category	INCOME	TITHE/GIVING	TAXES	HOUSING	FOOD	TRANSPORTATION	INSURANCE
BUDGETED AMOUNT	$ 4,440	$ 444	$ 900	$ 1,080	$ 338	$ 328	$ 83
Date							
1	2,000	200	450			22	
2				36			
3					32		
4							
5				780		36	
6							
7	20				7		
8							
9							
10	100	22				100	
11							30
12					64		
13				17			
14						8	
15							
This month SUBTOTAL	$ 2,120	$ 222	$ 450	$ 833	$ 103	$ 166	$ 30
16	2,000	200	450				
17						37	
18				21			
19	80			26	74		
20							
21						12	53
22							
23	135				37		
24				113			
25					52		
26	15	22			42		
27	200			107		138	
28							
29					20		
30							
31							
This month TOTAL	$ 4,550	$ 444	$ 900	$ 1,100	$ 328	$ 353	$ 83
This month SURPLUS/DEFICIT	$ 110	$ 0	$ 0	$ (20)	$ 10	$ (25)	$ 0
Year to Date BUDGET	$ 8,880	$ 888	$ 1800	$ 2160	$ 676	$ 656	$ 166
Year to Date TOTAL	$ 8,590	$ 694	$ 1735	$ 2201	$ 666	$ 721	$ 166
Year to Date SURPLUS/DEFICIT	$ (290)	$ 194	$ 65	$ (41)	$ 10	$ (65)	$ 0

BUDGET SUMMARY

This Month	Previous Month/Year to Date	Year to Date
Total Income $ 4,550	Total Income $ 4,040	Total Income $ 8,590
Minus Total Expenses $ 4,250	Minus Total Expenses $ 4,167	Minus Total Expenses $ 8,417
Equals Surplus/Deficit $ 300	Equals Surplus/Deficit $ (127)	Equals Surplus/Deficit $ 173

+ =

Don and Janet's Sample

50

Monthly Budget

Category	DEBTS	ENT./REC.	CLOTHING	SAVINGS	MEDICAL	MISCELLANEOUS	INVESTMENTS	SCHOOL/DAYCARE
BUDGETED AMOUNT	$ 154	$ 242	$ 94	$ 200	$ 40	$ 281	$ 40	$ 216
Date								
1				100				
2			22					
3						19		
4		19						
5								
6								200
7							20	
8		34				65		
9	20							
10	14							
11			19					
12					25			
13		26						
14								
15								
This month SUBTOTAL	$ 34	$ 79	$ 41	$ 100	$ 25	$ 84	$ 20	$ 200
16	100			100				
17		9				12		
18			8					
19								
20								
21						30		
22		54						
23								
24			10			40	20	
25					15			
26	20	2						
27								
28		17	9			13		
29								
30								
31								
This month TOTAL	$ 154	$ 161	$ 68	$ 200	$ 40	$ 179	$ 40	$ 200
This month SURPLUS/DEFICIT	$ 0	$ 81	$ 26	$ 0	$ 0	$ 102	$ 0	$ 16
Year to Date BUDGET	$ 308	$ 484	$ 188	$ 400	$ 80	$ 562	$ 80	$ 432
Year to Date TOTAL	$ 308	$ 403	$ 162	$ 365	$ 80	$ 460	$ 40	$ 416
Year to Date SURPLUS/DEFICIT	$ 0	$ 81	$ 26	$ 35	$ 0	$ 102	$ 40	$ 16

| Month   Year | | | | | | |

Monthly Budget

Category	INCOME	TITHE/GIVING	TAXES	HOUSING	FOOD	TRANSPORTATION	INSURANCE
BUDGETED AMOUNT	$	$	$	$	$	$	$
Date							
1							
2							
3							
4							
5							
6							
7							
8							
9							
10							
11							
12							
13							
14							
15							
This month SUBTOTAL	$	$	$	$	$	$	$
16							
17							
18							
19							
20							
21							
22							
23							
24							
25							
26							
27							
28							
29							
30							
31							
This month TOTAL	$	$	$	$	$	$	$
This month SURPLUS/DEFICIT	$	$	$	$	$	$	$
Year to Date BUDGET	$	$	$	$	$	$	$
Year to Date TOTAL	$	$	$	$	$	$	$
Year to Date SURPLUS/DEFICIT	$	$	$	$	$	$	$

BUDGET SUMMARY

This Month		Previous Month/Year to Date		Year to Date
Total Income $ _____		Total Income $ _____		Total Income $ _____
Minus Total Expenses $ _____	**+**	Minus Total Expenses $ _____	**=**	Minus Total Expenses $ _____
Equals Surplus/Deficit $ _____		Equals Surplus/Deficit $ _____		Equals Surplus/Deficit $ _____

Monthly Budget

Category	DEBTS	ENT./REC.	CLOTHING	SAVINGS	MEDICAL	MISCELLANEOUS	INVESTMENTS	SCHOOL/DAYCARE
BUDGETED AMOUNT	$	$	$	$	$	$	$	$
Date								
1								
2								
3								
4								
5								
6								
7								
8								
9								
10								
11								
12								
13								
14								
15								
This month SUBTOTAL	$	$	$	$	$	$	$	$
16								
17								
18								
19								
20								
21								
22								
23								
24								
25								
26								
27								
28								
29								
30								
31								
This month TOTAL	$	$	$	$	$	$	$	$
This month SURPLUS/DEFICIT	$	$	$	$	$	$	$	$
Year to Date BUDGET	$	$	$	$	$	$	$	$
Year to Date TOTAL	$	$	$	$	$	$	$	$
Year to Date SURPLUS/DEFICIT	$	$	$	$	$	$	$	$

Month	Year						

Monthly Budget

Category	INCOME	TITHE/GIVING	TAXES	HOUSING	FOOD	TRANSPORTATION	INSURANCE
BUDGETED AMOUNT	$	$	$	$	$	$	$
Date							
1							
2							
3							
4							
5							
6							
7							
8							
9							
10							
11							
12							
13							
14							
15							
This month SUBTOTAL	$	$	$	$	$	$	$
16							
17							
18							
19							
20							
21							
22							
23							
24							
25							
26							
27							
28							
29							
30							
31							
This month TOTAL	$	$	$	$	$	$	$
This month SURPLUS/DEFICIT	$	$	$	$	$	$	$
Year to Date BUDGET	$	$	$	$	$	$	$
Year to Date TOTAL	$	$	$	$	$	$	$
Year to Date SURPLUS/DEFICIT	$	$	$	$	$	$	$

BUDGET SUMMARY

This Month
Total Income $ _____
Minus Total Expenses $ _____
Equals Surplus/Deficit $ _____

+

Previous Month/Year to Date
Total Income $ _____
Minus Total Expenses $ _____
Equals Surplus/Deficit $ _____

=

Year to Date
Total Income $ _____
Minus Total Expenses $ _____
Equals Surplus/Deficit $ _____

Monthly Budget

Category	DEBTS	ENT./REC.	CLOTHING	SAVINGS	MEDICAL	MISCELLANEOUS	INVESTMENTS	SCHOOL/DAYCARE
BUDGETED AMOUNT	$	$	$	$	$	$	$	$
Date								
1								
2								
3								
4								
5								
6								
7								
8								
9								
10								
11								
12								
13								
14								
15								
This month SUBTOTAL	$	$	$	$	$	$	$	$
16								
17								
18								
19								
20								
21								
22								
23								
24								
25								
26								
27								
28								
29								
30								
31								
This month TOTAL	$	$	$	$	$	$	$	$
This month SURPLUS/DEFICIT	$	$	$	$	$	$	$	$
Year to Date BUDGET	$	$	$	$	$	$	$	$
Year to Date TOTAL	$	$	$	$	$	$	$	$
Year to Date SURPLUS/DEFICIT	$	$	$	$	$	$	$	$

Month	Year						

Monthly Budget

Category	INCOME	TITHE/GIVING	TAXES	HOUSING	FOOD	TRANSPORTATION	INSURANCE
BUDGETED AMOUNT	$	$	$	$	$	$	$
Date							
1							
2							
3							
4							
5							
6							
7							
8							
9							
10							
11							
12							
13							
14							
15							
This month SUBTOTAL	$	$	$	$	$	$	$
16							
17							
18							
19							
20							
21							
22							
23							
24							
25							
26							
27							
28							
29							
30							
31							
This month TOTAL	$	$	$	$	$	$	$
This month SURPLUS/DEFICIT	$	$	$	$	$	$	$
Year to Date BUDGET	$	$	$	$	$	$	$
Year to Date TOTAL	$	$	$	$	$	$	$
Year to Date SURPLUS/DEFICIT	$	$	$	$	$	$	$

BUDGET SUMMARY

This Month	Previous Month/Year to Date	Year to Date
Total Income $ _____	Total Income $ _____	Total Income $ _____
Minus Total Expenses $ _____	Minus Total Expenses $ _____	Minus Total Expenses $ _____
Equals Surplus/Deficit $ _____	Equals Surplus/Deficit $ _____	Equals Surplus/Deficit $ _____

This Month **+** Previous Month/Year to Date **=** Year to Date

Monthly Budget

Category	DEBTS	ENT./REC.	CLOTHING	SAVINGS	MEDICAL	MISCELLANEOUS	INVESTMENTS	SCHOOL/DAYCARE
BUDGETED AMOUNT	$	$	$	$	$	$	$	$
Date								
1								
2								
3								
4								
5								
6								
7								
8								
9								
10								
11								
12								
13								
14								
15								
This month SUBTOTAL	$	$	$	$	$	$	$	$
16								
17								
18								
19								
20								
21								
22								
23								
24								
25								
26								
27								
28								
29								
30								
31								
This month TOTAL	$	$	$	$	$	$	$	$
This month SURPLUS/DEFICIT	$	$	$	$	$	$	$	$
Year to Date BUDGET	$	$	$	$	$	$	$	$
Year to Date TOTAL	$	$	$	$	$	$	$	$
Year to Date SURPLUS/DEFICIT	$	$	$	$	$	$	$	$

Category	INCOME	TITHE/GIVING	TAXES	HOUSING	FOOD	TRANSPORTATION	INSURANCE
Month	**Year**			**Monthly Budget**			
BUDGETED AMOUNT	$	$	$	$	$	$	$
Date							
1							
2							
3							
4							
5							
6							
7							
8							
9							
10							
11							
12							
13							
14							
15							
This month SUBTOTAL	$	$	$	$	$	$	$
16							
17							
18							
19							
20							
21							
22							
23							
24							
25							
26							
27							
28							
29							
30							
31							
This month TOTAL	$	$	$	$	$	$	$
This month SURPLUS/DEFICIT	$	$	$	$	$	$	$
Year to Date BUDGET	$	$	$	$	$	$	$
Year to Date TOTAL	$	$	$	$	$	$	$
Year to Date SURPLUS/DEFICIT	$	$	$	$	$	$	$

BUDGET SUMMARY

This Month	Previous Month/Year to Date	Year to Date
Total Income $ _____	Total Income $ _____	Total Income $ _____
Minus Total Expenses $ _____	Minus Total Expenses $ _____	Minus Total Expenses $ _____
Equals Surplus/Deficit $ _____	Equals Surplus/Deficit $ _____	Equals Surplus/Deficit $ _____

+ **=**

Monthly Budget

Category	DEBTS	ENT./REC.	CLOTHING	SAVINGS	MEDICAL	MISCELLANEOUS	INVESTMENTS	SCHOOL/DAYCARE
BUDGETED AMOUNT	$	$	$	$	$	$	$	$
Date								
1								
2								
3								
4								
5								
6								
7								
8								
9								
10								
11								
12								
13								
14								
15								
This month SUBTOTAL	$	$	$	$	$	$	$	$
16								
17								
18								
19								
20								
21								
22								
23								
24								
25								
26								
27								
28								
29								
30								
31								
This month TOTAL	$	$	$	$	$	$	$	$
This month SURPLUS/DEFICIT	$	$	$	$	$	$	$	$
Year to Date BUDGET	$	$	$	$	$	$	$	$
Year to Date TOTAL	$	$	$	$	$	$	$	$
Year to Date SURPLUS/DEFICIT	$	$	$	$	$	$	$	$

Monthly Budget

Category	INCOME	TITHE/GIVING	TAXES	HOUSING	FOOD	TRANSPORTATION	INSURANCE
BUDGETED AMOUNT	$	$	$	$	$	$	$
Date							
1							
2							
3							
4							
5							
6							
7							
8							
9							
10							
11							
12							
13							
14							
15							
This month SUBTOTAL	$	$	$	$	$	$	$
16							
17							
18							
19							
20							
21							
22							
23							
24							
25							
26							
27							
28							
29							
30							
31							
This month TOTAL	$	$	$	$	$	$	$
This month SURPLUS/DEFICIT	$	$	$	$	$	$	$
Year to Date BUDGET	$	$	$	$	$	$	$
Year to Date TOTAL	$	$	$	$	$	$	$
Year to Date SURPLUS/DEFICIT	$	$	$	$	$	$	$

BUDGET SUMMARY

This Month		Previous Month/Year to Date		Year to Date
Total Income $ _____		Total Income $ _____		Total Income $ _____
Minus Total Expenses $ _____	**+**	Minus Total Expenses $ _____	**=**	Minus Total Expenses $ _____
Equals Surplus/Deficit $ _____		Equals Surplus/Deficit $ _____		Equals Surplus/Deficit $ _____

Monthly Budget

Category	DEBTS	ENT./REC.	CLOTHING	SAVINGS	MEDICAL	MISCELLANEOUS	INVESTMENTS	SCHOOL/DAYCARE
BUDGETED AMOUNT	$	$	$	$	$	$	$	$
Date								
1								
2								
3								
4								
5								
6								
7								
8								
9								
10								
11								
12								
13								
14								
15								
This month SUBTOTAL	$	$	$	$	$	$	$	$
16								
17								
18								
19								
20								
21								
22								
23								
24								
25								
26								
27								
28								
29								
30								
31								
This month TOTAL	$	$	$	$	$	$	$	$
This month SURPLUS/DEFICIT	$	$	$	$	$	$	$	$
Year to Date BUDGET	$	$	$	$	$	$	$	$
Year to Date TOTAL	$	$	$	$	$	$	$	$
Year to Date SURPLUS/DEFICIT	$	$	$	$	$	$	$	$

Month	Year			**Monthly Budget**			

Category	INCOME	TITHE/GIVING	TAXES	HOUSING	FOOD	TRANSPORTATION	INSURANCE
BUDGETED AMOUNT	$	$	$	$	$	$	$
Date							
1							
2							
3							
4							
5							
6							
7							
8							
9							
10							
11							
12							
13							
14							
15							
This month SUBTOTAL	$	$	$	$	$	$	$
16							
17							
18							
19							
20							
21							
22							
23							
24							
25							
26							
27							
28							
29							
30							
31							
This month TOTAL	$	$	$	$	$	$	$
This month SURPLUS/DEFICIT	$	$	$	$	$	$	$
Year to Date BUDGET	$	$	$	$	$	$	$
Year to Date TOTAL	$	$	$	$	$	$	$
Year to Date SURPLUS/DEFICIT	$	$	$	$	$	$	$

BUDGET SUMMARY

This Month
Total Income $ _____
Minus Total Expenses $ _____
Equals Surplus/Deficit $ _____

+

Previous Month/Year to Date
Total Income $ _____
Minus Total Expenses $ _____
Equals Surplus/Deficit $ _____

=

Year to Date
Total Income $ _____
Minus Total Expenses $ _____
Equals Surplus/Deficit $ _____

Monthly Budget

Category	DEBTS	ENT./REC.	CLOTHING	SAVINGS	MEDICAL	MISCELLANEOUS	INVESTMENTS	SCHOOL/DAYCARE
BUDGETED AMOUNT	$	$	$	$	$	$	$	$
Date								
1								
2								
3								
4								
5								
6								
7								
8								
9								
10								
11								
12								
13								
14								
15								
This month SUBTOTAL	$	$	$	$	$	$	$	$
16								
17								
18								
19								
20								
21								
22								
23								
24								
25								
26								
27								
28								
29								
30								
31								
This month TOTAL	$	$	$	$	$	$	$	$
This month SURPLUS/DEFICIT	$	$	$	$	$	$	$	$
Year to Date BUDGET	$	$	$	$	$	$	$	$
Year to Date TOTAL	$	$	$	$	$	$	$	$
Year to Date SURPLUS/DEFICIT	$	$	$	$	$	$	$	$

Monthly Budget

Category	INCOME	TITHE/GIVING	TAXES	HOUSING	FOOD	TRANSPORTATION	INSURANCE
BUDGETED AMOUNT	$	$	$	$	$	$	$
Date							
1							
2							
3							
4							
5							
6							
7							
8							
9							
10							
11							
12							
13							
14							
15							
This month SUBTOTAL	$	$	$	$	$	$	$
16							
17							
18							
19							
20							
21							
22							
23							
24							
25							
26							
27							
28							
29							
30							
31							
This month TOTAL	$	$	$	$	$	$	$
This month SURPLUS/DEFICIT	$	$	$	$	$	$	$
Year to Date BUDGET	$	$	$	$	$	$	$
Year to Date TOTAL	$	$	$	$	$	$	$
Year to Date SURPLUS/DEFICIT	$	$	$	$	$	$	$

BUDGET SUMMARY

This Month	Previous Month/Year to Date	Year to Date
Total Income $ _____	Total Income $ _____	Total Income $ _____
Minus Total Expenses $ _____	Minus Total Expenses $ _____	Minus Total Expenses $ _____
Equals Surplus/Deficit $ _____	Equals Surplus/Deficit $ _____	Equals Surplus/Deficit $ _____

+ =

Monthly Budget

Category	DEBTS	ENT./REC.	CLOTHING	SAVINGS	MEDICAL	MISCELLANEOUS	INVESTMENTS	SCHOOL/DAYCARE
BUDGETED AMOUNT	$	$	$	$	$	$	$	$
Date								
1								
2								
3								
4								
5								
6								
7								
8								
9								
10								
11								
12								
13								
14								
15								
This month SUBTOTAL	$	$	$	$	$	$	$	$
16								
17								
18								
19								
20								
21								
22								
23								
24								
25								
26								
27								
28								
29								
30								
31								
This month TOTAL	$	$	$	$	$	$	$	$
This month SURPLUS/DEFICIT	$	$	$	$	$	$	$	$
Year to Date BUDGET	$	$	$	$	$	$	$	$
Year to Date TOTAL	$	$	$	$	$	$	$	$
Year to Date SURPLUS/DEFICIT	$	$	$	$	$	$	$	$

Month	Year						

Monthly Budget

Category	INCOME	TITHE/GIVING	TAXES	HOUSING	FOOD	TRANSPORTATION	INSURANCE
BUDGETED AMOUNT	$	$	$	$	$	$	$
Date							
1							
2							
3							
4							
5							
6							
7							
8							
9							
10							
11							
12							
13							
14							
15							
This month SUBTOTAL	$	$	$	$	$	$	$
16							
17							
18							
19							
20							
21							
22							
23							
24							
25							
26							
27							
28							
29							
30							
31							
This month TOTAL	$	$	$	$	$	$	$
This month SURPLUS/DEFICIT	$	$	$	$	$	$	$
Year to Date BUDGET	$	$	$	$	$	$	$
Year to Date TOTAL	$	$	$	$	$	$	$
Year to Date SURPLUS/DEFICIT	$	$	$	$	$	$	$

BUDGET SUMMARY

This Month
Total Income $ _____
Minus Total Expenses $ _____
Equals Surplus/Deficit $ _____

+

Previous Month/Year to Date
Total Income $ _____
Minus Total Expenses $ _____
Equals Surplus/Deficit $ _____

=

Year to Date
Total Income $ _____
Minus Total Expenses $ _____
Equals Surplus/Deficit $ _____

Monthly Budget

Category	DEBTS	ENT./REC.	CLOTHING	SAVINGS	MEDICAL	MISCELLANEOUS	INVESTMENTS	SCHOOL/DAYCARE
BUDGETED AMOUNT	$	$	$	$	$	$	$	$
Date								
1								
2								
3								
4								
5								
6								
7								
8								
9								
10								
11								
12								
13								
14								
15								
This month SUBTOTAL	$	$	$	$	$	$	$	$
16								
17								
18								
19								
20								
21								
22								
23								
24								
25								
26								
27								
28								
29								
30								
31								
This month TOTAL	$	$	$	$	$	$	$	$
This month SURPLUS/DEFICIT	$	$	$	$	$	$	$	$
Year to Date BUDGET	$	$	$	$	$	$	$	$
Year to Date TOTAL	$	$	$	$	$	$	$	$
Year to Date SURPLUS/DEFICIT	$	$	$	$	$	$	$	$

Month	Year						

Monthly Budget

Category	INCOME	TITHE/GIVING	TAXES	HOUSING	FOOD	TRANSPORTATION	INSURANCE
BUDGETED AMOUNT	$	$	$	$	$	$	$
Date							
1							
2							
3							
4							
5							
6							
7							
8							
9							
10							
11							
12							
13							
14							
15							
This month SUBTOTAL	$	$	$	$	$	$	$
16							
17							
18							
19							
20							
21							
22							
23							
24							
25							
26							
27							
28							
29							
30							
31							
This month TOTAL	$	$	$	$	$	$	$
This month SURPLUS/DEFICIT	$	$	$	$	$	$	$
Year to Date BUDGET	$	$	$	$	$	$	$
Year to Date TOTAL	$	$	$	$	$	$	$
Year to Date SURPLUS/DEFICIT	$	$	$	$	$	$	$

BUDGET SUMMARY

This Month		Previous Month/Year to Date		Year to Date
Total Income $ _____		Total Income $ _____		Total Income $ _____
Minus Total Expenses $ _____	**+**	Minus Total Expenses $ _____	**=**	Minus Total Expenses $ _____
Equals Surplus/Deficit $ _____		Equals Surplus/Deficit $ _____		Equals Surplus/Deficit $ _____

Monthly Budget

Category	DEBTS	ENT./REC.	CLOTHING	SAVINGS	MEDICAL	MISCELLANEOUS	INVESTMENTS	SCHOOL/DAYCARE
BUDGETED AMOUNT	$	$	$	$	$	$	$	$
Date								
1								
2								
3								
4								
5								
6								
7								
8								
9								
10								
11								
12								
13								
14								
15								
This month SUBTOTAL	$	$	$	$	$	$	$	$
16								
17								
18								
19								
20								
21								
22								
23								
24								
25								
26								
27								
28								
29								
30								
31								
This month TOTAL	$	$	$	$	$	$	$	$
This month SURPLUS/DEFICIT	$	$	$	$	$	$	$	$
Year to Date BUDGET	$	$	$	$	$	$	$	$
Year to Date TOTAL	$	$	$	$	$	$	$	$
Year to Date SURPLUS/DEFICIT	$	$	$	$	$	$	$	$

Monthly Budget

Category	INCOME	TITHE/GIVING	TAXES	HOUSING	FOOD	TRANSPORTATION	INSURANCE
BUDGETED AMOUNT	$	$	$	$	$	$	$
Date							
1							
2							
3							
4							
5							
6							
7							
8							
9							
10							
11							
12							
13							
14							
15							
This month SUBTOTAL	$	$	$	$	$	$	$
16							
17							
18							
19							
20							
21							
22							
23							
24							
25							
26							
27							
28							
29							
30							
31							
This month TOTAL	$	$	$	$	$	$	$
This month SURPLUS/DEFICIT	$	$	$	$	$	$	$
Year to Date BUDGET	$	$	$	$	$	$	$
Year to Date TOTAL	$	$	$	$	$	$	$
Year to Date SURPLUS/DEFICIT	$	$	$	$	$	$	$

BUDGET SUMMARY

This Month		Previous Month/Year to Date		Year to Date
Total Income $ _____		Total Income $ _____		Total Income $ _____
Minus Total Expenses $ _____	**+**	Minus Total Expenses $ _____	**=**	Minus Total Expenses $ _____
Equals Surplus/Deficit $ _____		Equals Surplus/Deficit $ _____		Equals Surplus/Deficit $ _____

Monthly Budget

Category	DEBTS	ENT./REC.	CLOTHING	SAVINGS	MEDICAL	MISCELLANEOUS	INVESTMENTS	SCHOOL/DAYCARE
BUDGETED AMOUNT	$	$	$	$	$	$	$	$
Date								
1								
2								
3								
4								
5								
6								
7								
8								
9								
10								
11								
12								
13								
14								
15								
This month SUBTOTAL	$	$	$	$	$	$	$	$
16								
17								
18								
19								
20								
21								
22								
23								
24								
25								
26								
27								
28								
29								
30								
31								
This month TOTAL	$	$	$	$	$	$	$	$
This month SURPLUS/DEFICIT	$	$	$	$	$	$	$	$
Year to Date BUDGET	$	$	$	$	$	$	$	$
Year to Date TOTAL	$	$	$	$	$	$	$	$
Year to Date SURPLUS/DEFICIT	$	$	$	$	$	$	$	$

Month		Year		Monthly Budget			

Category	INCOME	TITHE/GIVING	TAXES	HOUSING	FOOD	TRANSPORTATION	INSURANCE
BUDGETED AMOUNT	$	$	$	$	$	$	$
Date							
1							
2							
3							
4							
5							
6							
7							
8							
9							
10							
11							
12							
13							
14							
15							
This month SUBTOTAL	$	$	$	$	$	$	$
16							
17							
18							
19							
20							
21							
22							
23							
24							
25							
26							
27							
28							
29							
30							
31							
This month TOTAL	$	$	$	$	$	$	$
This month SURPLUS/DEFICIT	$	$	$	$	$	$	$
Year to Date BUDGET	$	$	$	$	$	$	$
Year to Date TOTAL	$	$	$	$	$	$	$
Year to Date SURPLUS/DEFICIT	$	$	$	$	$	$	$

BUDGET SUMMARY

This Month
Total Income $ _____
Minus Total Expenses $ _____
Equals Surplus/Deficit $ _____

+

Previous Month/Year to Date
Total Income $ _____
Minus Total Expenses $ _____
Equals Surplus/Deficit $ _____

=

Year to Date
Total Income $ _____
Minus Total Expenses $ _____
Equals Surplus/Deficit $ _____

Monthly Budget

Category	DEBTS	ENT./REC.	CLOTHING	SAVINGS	MEDICAL	MISCELLANEOUS	INVESTMENTS	SCHOOL/DAYCARE
BUDGETED AMOUNT	$	$	$	$	$	$	$	$
Date								
1								
2								
3								
4								
5								
6								
7								
8								
9								
10								
11								
12								
13								
14								
15								
This month SUBTOTAL	$	$	$	$	$	$	$	$
16								
17								
18								
19								
20								
21								
22								
23								
24								
25								
26								
27								
28								
29								
30								
31								
This month TOTAL	$	$	$	$	$	$	$	$
This month SURPLUS/DEFICIT	$	$	$	$	$	$	$	$
Year to Date BUDGET	$	$	$	$	$	$	$	$
Year to Date TOTAL	$	$	$	$	$	$	$	$
Year to Date SURPLUS/DEFICIT	$	$	$	$	$	$	$	$

Monthly Budget

Category	INCOME	TITHE/GIVING	TAXES	HOUSING	FOOD	TRANSPORTATION	INSURANCE
BUDGETED AMOUNT	$	$	$	$	$	$	$
Date							
1							
2							
3							
4							
5							
6							
7							
8							
9							
10							
11							
12							
13							
14							
15							
This month SUBTOTAL	$	$	$	$	$	$	$
16							
17							
18							
19							
20							
21							
22							
23							
24							
25							
26							
27							
28							
29							
30							
31							
This month TOTAL	$	$	$	$	$	$	$
This month SURPLUS/DEFICIT	$	$	$	$	$	$	$
Year to Date BUDGET	$	$	$	$	$	$	$
Year to Date TOTAL	$	$	$	$	$	$	$
Year to Date SURPLUS/DEFICIT	$	$	$	$	$	$	$

BUDGET SUMMARY

This Month		Previous Month/Year to Date		Year to Date
Total Income $ _____		Total Income $ _____		Total Income $ _____
Minus Total Expenses $ _____	**+**	Minus Total Expenses $ _____	**=**	Minus Total Expenses $ _____
Equals Surplus/Deficit $ _____		Equals Surplus/Deficit $ _____		Equals Surplus/Deficit $ _____

Monthly Budget

Category	DEBTS	ENT./REC.	CLOTHING	SAVINGS	MEDICAL	MISCELLANEOUS	INVESTMENTS	SCHOOL/DAYCARE
BUDGETED AMOUNT	$	$	$	$	$	$	$	$
Date								
1								
2								
3								
4								
5								
6								
7								
8								
9								
10								
11								
12								
13								
14								
15								
This month SUBTOTAL	$	$	$	$	$	$	$	$
16								
17								
18								
19								
20								
21								
22								
23								
24								
25								
26								
27								
28								
29								
30								
31								
This month TOTAL	$	$	$	$	$	$	$	$
This month SURPLUS/DEFICIT	$	$	$	$	$	$	$	$
Year to Date BUDGET	$	$	$	$	$	$	$	$
Year to Date TOTAL	$	$	$	$	$	$	$	$
Year to Date SURPLUS/DEFICIT	$	$	$	$	$	$	$	$

Monthly Budget

Month	Year

Category	INCOME	TITHE/GIVING	TAXES	HOUSING	FOOD	TRANSPORTATION	INSURANCE
BUDGETED AMOUNT	$	$	$	$	$	$	$
Date							
1							
2							
3							
4							
5							
6							
7							
8							
9							
10							
11							
12							
13							
14							
15							
This month SUBTOTAL	$	$	$	$	$	$	$
16							
17							
18							
19							
20							
21							
22							
23							
24							
25							
26							
27							
28							
29							
30							
31							
This month TOTAL	$	$	$	$	$	$	$
This month SURPLUS/DEFICIT	$	$	$	$	$	$	$
Year to Date BUDGET	$	$	$	$	$	$	$
Year to Date TOTAL	$	$	$	$	$	$	$
Year to Date SURPLUS/DEFICIT	$	$	$	$	$	$	$

BUDGET SUMMARY

This Month		Previous Month/Year to Date		Year to Date
Total Income $ _____		Total Income $ _____		Total Income $ _____
Minus Total Expenses $ _____	**+**	Minus Total Expenses $ _____	**=**	Minus Total Expenses $ _____
Equals Surplus/Deficit $ _____		Equals Surplus/Deficit $ _____		Equals Surplus/Deficit $ _____

Monthly Budget

Category	DEBTS	ENT./REC.	CLOTHING	SAVINGS	MEDICAL	MISCELLANEOUS	INVESTMENTS	SCHOOL/DAYCARE
BUDGETED AMOUNT	$	$	$	$	$	$	$	$
Date								
1								
2								
3								
4								
5								
6								
7								
8								
9								
10								
11								
12								
13								
14								
15								
This month SUBTOTAL	$	$	$	$	$	$	$	$
16								
17								
18								
19								
20								
21								
22								
23								
24								
25								
26								
27								
28								
29								
30								
31								
This month TOTAL	$	$	$	$	$	$	$	$
This month SURPLUS/DEFICIT	$	$	$	$	$	$	$	$
Year to Date BUDGET	$	$	$	$	$	$	$	$
Year to Date TOTAL	$	$	$	$	$	$	$	$
Year to Date SURPLUS/DEFICIT	$	$	$	$	$	$	$	$

Category Page

(Individual Account Page)

SPENDING CATEGORY

DATE	CK. #	TRANSACTION	DEPOSIT		WITHDRAWAL		BALANCE	

Category Page

(Individual Account Page)

_____

SPENDING CATEGORY

DATE	CK. #	TRANSACTION	DEPOSIT		WITHDRAWAL		BALANCE	

Category Page

(Individual Account Page)

_____
SPENDING CATEGORY

DATE	CK. #	TRANSACTION	DEPOSIT		WITHDRAWAL		BALANCE	

Category Page
(Individual Account Page)

SPENDING CATEGORY

DATE	CK. #	TRANSACTION	DEPOSIT	WITHDRAWAL	BALANCE

Category Page
(Individual Account Page)

_____

SPENDING CATEGORY

DATE	CK. #	TRANSACTION	DEPOSIT		WITHDRAWAL		BALANCE	

Category Page

(Individual Account Page)

SPENDING CATEGORY

DATE	CK. #	TRANSACTION	DEPOSIT		WITHDRAWAL		BALANCE	

This week we will focus on your checking account, because many people have only a vague idea of how much is in their accounts and do not regularly balance their checkbooks. We will also explore several helpful budgeting hints.

YOUR CHECKING ACCOUNT

1. THE BEGINNING BALANCE

The current balance in your checkbook is the beginning balance. In Don and Janet's example below, they opened a new account and their initial deposit was Don's salary.

2. RECORDING TRANSACTIONS

Deposit all your income into your checking account and record each transaction in the checking account register. Examine Don and Janet's register:

DATE	CHECK NUMBER	CHECKS ISSUED TO OR DEPOSIT RECEIVED FROM	AMOUNT OF DEPOSIT	✓	AMOUNT OF CHECK	BALANCE
1/1	DEP.	Don's Salary	2,000.00	✓		2,000.00
1/1	101	First Church		✓	200.00	1,800.00
1/1	102	Savings			100.00	1,700.00
1/3	103	Good Gas Station			35.00	1,665.00
		(Car Repair)				
1/4	104	Best Grocery Store			50.00	1,615.00
1/5	105	Second Natl. Bank			780.00	835.00

Each deposit (all income) and each check written (all spending) is entered and described. Take as many lines as you need to describe each transaction. Maintain a running balance so you will always know how much money remains in your checking account.

☐ **For Checks Written or Automatic Withdrawals**
Record the date, check number, description, and amount of the check. Then subtract the amount of the check or automatic withdrawal from the existing balance to determine the new balance.

☐ **For Deposits Made**
Record the date, write the abbreviation for deposit—DEP—in the "Check Number" column, describe the source of income, and the amount of the deposit. Then add the amount of the deposit to your balance.

You must balance (reconcile) your monthly bank statement with your checkbook register to verify that neither you nor the bank have committed an error. This is important. An inaccurate balance can result in an overdrawn account and expensive bank charges.

Balance your checkbook as soon as you receive the statement by completing the following steps:

Step 1: Compare the information on each check and deposit with the entry in your checkbook register and with the balance statement. If all these agree, place a check mark (✔) in the proper column. In Don and Janet's example on the previous page, they have verified the first deposit and check number 101. A check mark has been placed in the checkbook register to confirm that each transaction is correct. Remember to add interest earned and deduct service charges in your checkbook.

Step 2: Complete the following:

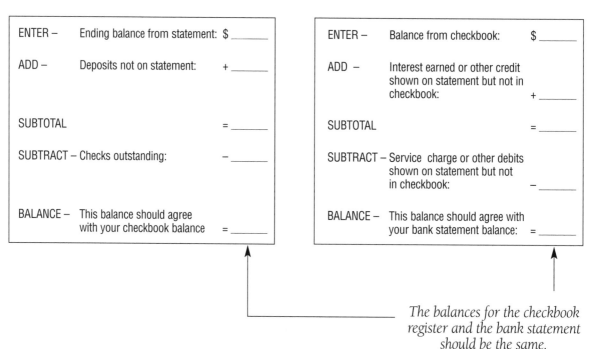

In your Bank Statement

ENTER –	Ending balance from statement:	$ _____
ADD –	Deposits not on statement:	+ _____
SUBTOTAL		= _____
SUBTRACT –	Checks outstanding:	– _____
BALANCE –	This balance should agree with your checkbook balance	= _____

In your Checkbook Register

ENTER –	Balance from checkbook:	$ _____
ADD –	Interest earned or other credit shown on statement but not in checkbook:	+ _____
SUBTOTAL		= _____
SUBTRACT –	Service charge or other debits shown on statement but not in checkbook:	– _____
BALANCE –	This balance should agree with your bank statement balance:	= _____

The balances for the checkbook register and the bank statement should be the same.

Step 3: Compare the new Checkbook Register balance with that of the bank statement. They should be the same. Never allow the Checkbook Register and the bank statement to disagree in balance. The most common mistakes are arithmetic errors. Using a printing calculator will help avoid these mistakes because it enables you to check your calculator entries against the original figures. If you use a budgeting software program, your arithmetic errors will also be reduced.

BUDGETING HINTS

1. Housing

Because homes have become so expensive, housing often throws the entire budget out of balance. As a rough rule of thumb, you probably cannot afford a house costing more than 1.7 times your annual gross income. This assumes that you take out a mortgage for about 85% of the cost of the home. For example, Don and Janet would multiply their gross annual income of $53,280 a year by 1.7 to calculate that they could afford to purchase a $90,500 house.

If your house costs more than 1.7 times your gross annual income, your total spending for the housing category (including insurance, utilities, maintenance, real estate taxes, etc.) will probably exceed the recommended percentage guide. You will need to reduce spending in other categories to balance your budget.

2. Gifts

A major budget-buster for many people is overspending on gifts. Tradition dictates a gift for nearly every occasion. The amount of money spent on gifts is often underestimated. When you completed your Estimated Budget earlier in the study, you estimated the amount of money spent on gifts. Because gift spending is so important to control, spend some more time and more accurately estimate your spending by completing the following:

Christmas presents	$ _____
Birthdays	$ _____
Anniversaries	$ _____
Weddings	$ _____
Graduation gifts	$ _____
Office gifts	$ _____
Total Gifts	$ _____

To bring the cost of gifts under control, consider: (1) Keeping an event calendar for the year and budgeting ahead; (2) Determining not to buy gifts on credit, especially Christmas gifts; (3) Making some of the gifts; and (4) Drawing family names for selected gifts rather than giving to everyone.

3. Automatic Banking

Automatic withdrawals or deposits create additional challenges to maintain an accurate balance. Automatic withdrawals must be subtracted from the Checkbook Register at the time they are paid by the bank.

4. One Bookkeeper
When more than one individual attempts to maintain the record system, confusion usually results. If you are married, either the husband or the wife can keep the records. The choice should be based on who can do the job best.

5. Paid Every Two Weeks
If you are paid every two weeks rather than twice monthly, you will have two extra paychecks a year. It is recommended that those paychecks be used to fund some of the non-monthly expenses such as car repair, vacation, and clothing. The same would be true of tax refunds, bonuses, and gifts.

6. Automatic Overdrafts
Many banks offer an automatic overdraft protection service. If you write a check in excess of what you have in your account, the bank will still honor it. On the surface this looks like a helpful service. However, overdraft protection tends to create a complacent attitude about balancing the account and encourages overdrafting. Since these charges are accrued to a credit account, you will end up paying interest on your overdrafts. We recommend that these services be avoided.

7. Discipline
In order to provide the necessary control, you must discipline yourself to spend money based on the balance of the Monthly Budget and not based on the balance of the checkbook.

8. Keep It Simple
Don't try to make the record-keeping more complicated than necessary. This system should require no more than thirty minutes per week to maintain. If you choose to develop more detailed breakdowns of expenses and savings, wait until the budget has been in use for several months.

9. Checking Account Expenses
If a service charge is assessed to your checking account, record this as an expense in your checkbook register and as an expense under the Miscellaneous column.

10. Cash Organizer
Keeping track of cash is often the most challenging part of budgeting. The *Cash Organizer™ Envelope Budgeting System* will help you by tracking the cash portion of your spending.

Someone once said that the average person will work 40 years to accumulate assets, about 10 years conserving what he or she has accumulated, but no more than two hours planning for its ultimate distribution. Approximately seven out of ten people die without a will. To die without a will has four major drawbacks.

    1. The state laws will dictate who receives your assets. For instance, in many states a wife would receive only one-third to one-half of the husband's estate with the children (even adult children) receiving the rest. Married couples without children are often surprised to learn that many states give their parents or siblings as much as half of a person's estate.

    2. The heirs will face more cumbersome court proceedings and added legal fees.

    3. The estate may be subjected to higher taxes than would have been paid with wise estate planning.

    4. Tragically, under some circumstances the court can appoint a guardian (who may not know the Lord) to raise your children if you have not made this provision in your will.

    The person who knows Christ has a solemn duty to provide for his family. *"But if anyone does not provide for his own, and especially for those of his household, he has denied the faith, and is worse than an unbeliever"*(1 Timothy 5:8). This requirement extends to the responsibility of planning for the future of your loved ones should you predecease them.

    People avoid making a will for any of four reasons: (1) reluctance to face death; (2) procrastination; (3) they believe they have too little property; and (4) the expense of drafting a will.

    Whether you are married or single, rich or poor, you should have a will and complete the Organizing Your Estate worksheet. As Isaiah told Hezekiah, *"Thus says the Lord, 'Set your house in order, for you shall die'"* (2 Kings 20:1). Someday (should the Lord tarry) you will die. One of the greatest gifts you can leave your family for that emotional time will be an organized estate. Thirty-six percent die before retirement, so do not delay in preparing your will just because you are young. An increasingly popular option to the traditional will is a revocable living trust. Please seek competent legal and tax counsel before you decide which instrument is most suitable for you to use.

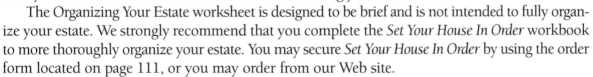

    Complete the Organizing Your Estate worksheet and review the information carefully with your spouse or heirs. After their review, give a completed copy to your attorney or accountant and a trusted family member or friend who will be involved in settling your estate.

    The Organizing Your Estate worksheet is designed to be brief and is not intended to fully organize your estate. We strongly recommend that you complete the *Set Your House In Order* workbook to more thoroughly organize your estate. You may secure *Set Your House In Order* by using the order form located on page 111, or you may order from our Web site.

Date: __January 1__

WILL AND/OR TRUST

The Will (Trust) is located: __David Smart's office__

The person designated to carry out its provisions is: __Janet__

If that person cannot or will not serve, the alternate is: __Mr. James Faithful__

Attorney: __David Smart__   Phone: __321-1000__

Accountant: __Gerry Numbers__   Phone: __432-4000__

INCOME BENEFITS

1. Company Benefits:
My/our heirs will begin receiving company benefits as follows: __One-third regular wage__

Contact: __Personnel Department__   Phone: __786-4545__

2. Social Security Benefits:
To receive Social Security benefits, go in person to the Social Security office located at:
__Orlando, Florida__

This should be done promptly because a delay may void some of the benefits. When you go take the following: (1) my Social Security card; (2) my death certificate; (3) your birth certificate; (4) our marriage certificate; (5) birth certificates for each child.

3. Veterans' Benefits:
You are/are not eligible for veterans' benefits: __Are not__

To receive these benefits you should do the following: _____

4. Life insurance coverage:
Insurance company: __Good Insurance Co.__   Policy #: __563-777__

Face Value: __$150,000__   Person insured: __Don__   Beneficiary: __Janet__

Insurance company: __Solid Insurance Co.__   Policy #: __838-776__

Face Value: __$50,000__   Person insured: __Janet__   Beneficiary: __Don__

Insurance company: _____   Policy #: _____

Face Value: _____   Person insured: _____   Beneficiary: _____

FAMILY INFORMATION

Family member's name:

Don   Address: 12 Nice Ave., Pleasantville

Social Security #: 123-45-6789

Janet   Address: 12 Nice Ave., Pleasantville

Social Security #: 234-56-7890

John   Address: 12 Nice Ave., Pleasantville

Social Security #: 345-67-8901

Ruth   Address: 12 Nice Ave., Pleasantville

Social Security #: 456-78-9012

Address:

Social Security #:

MILITARY SERVICE HISTORY

Branch of Service: Navy   Service number: 9876543

Length of Service: 3 years   From: 5/17/80   Until: 4/20/83

Rank: First Class (E-6)   Location and description of important military documents:

Honorable discharge in the cabinet at home

FUNERAL INSTRUCTIONS

Funeral Home: King's Funeral   Address: 325 Orange St.

Orlando, Florida   Phone: 645-3000

My/our place of burial is located at: Wood Lawn Memorial Gardens

You request burial in the following manner: A closed casket

You request that memorial gifts be given to the following church/organization:

First Church   Address: 400 Main St.

Food for the Poor Ministries   Address: 200 Second Ave.

Date: _____

WILL AND/OR TRUST

The Will (Trust) is located: _____

The person designated to carry out its provisions is: _____

If that person cannot or will not serve, the alternate is: _____

Attorney: _____ Phone: _____

Accountant: _____ Phone: _____

INCOME BENEFITS

1. Company Benefits:
My/our heirs will begin receiving company benefits as follows: _____
_____

Contact: _____ Phone: _____

2. Social Security Benefits:
To receive Social Security benefits, go in person to the Social Security office located at:
_____

This should be done promptly because a delay may void some of the benefits. When you go take the following: (1) my Social Security card; (2) my death certificate; (3) your birth certificate; (4) our marriage certificate; (5) birth certificates for each child.

3. Veterans' Benefits:
You are/are not eligible for veterans' benefits: _____

To receive these benefits you should do the following: _____
_____

4. Life insurance coverage:

Insurance company: _____ Policy #: _____

Face Value: _____ Person insured: _____ Beneficiary: _____

Insurance company: _____ Policy #: _____

Face Value: _____ Person insured: _____ Beneficiary: _____

Insurance company: _____ Policy #: _____

Face Value: _____ Person insured: _____ Beneficiary: _____

FAMILY INFORMATION

Family member's name:

_____ Address: _____

_____ Social Security #:_____

_____ Address: _____

_____ Social Security #:_____

_____ Address: _____

_____ Social Security #:_____

_____ Address: _____

_____ Social Security #:_____

_____ Address: _____

Social Security #:_____

MILITARY SERVICE HISTORY

Branch of Service:_____ Service number:_____

Length of Service:_____ From:_____ Until:_____

Rank:_____ Location and description of important military documents:

_____

_____

FUNERAL INSTRUCTIONS

Funeral Home: _____ Address: _____

_____ Phone: _____

My/our place of burial is located at: _____

_____

You request burial in the following manner:_____

_____

You request that memorial gifts be given to the following church/organization:

_____ Address:_____

_____ Address:_____

ORGANIZING YOUR INSURANCE & FILING SYSTEM

ORGANIZING YOUR INSURANCE

There are many types of insurance. Some of the most common are: homeowner's, automobile, liability, life, health, disability, and business.

The amount and type of insurance you carry will be dictated by your needs and your budget. Many cannot afford to purchase all the insurance they may need. If you are in this situation, prayerfully determine what insurance you can afford and which type you should purchase initially.

Because insurance can be complex and difficult to understand, seek experienced counsel when making your insurance decisions.

This week's practical application has a brief discussion about health and life insurance and a life insurance analysis for you to complete.

Health Insurance
Health insurance pays for doctor, hospital and other related expenses. The cost of health care, particularly if there is a major illness, can be very expensive. It is important to have health insurance if at all possible.

Life Insurance
The purpose of life insurance is to provide for the survivors' living expenses and lump-sum needs should a bread winner die. A lump-sum need is any debt, educational expense or other obligation that would not be a normal recurring expense that you would like to fund or pay off. The first step in deciding how much insurance to carry is to determine your total life insurance needs.

COMPLETING THE LIFE INSURANCE WORKSHEET

Complete the Life Insurance Worksheet on page 97 to get a rough approximation of your life insurance needs. *This is not intended to be precise. It does not take into consideration the impact inflation may have.* Seek the counsel of an expert to determine your needs accurately.

Present Annual Income Needs
Enter the amount of your yearly balanced budget.

Subtract Deceased Person's Needs
Expenses should drop as a result of the death of the breadwinner. For example, a second car may no longer be required, income taxes may be reduced, and less food will be consumed.

Subtract Income Available
Enter the amount of income the survivors will receive from all sources, such as Social Security, investments, retirement benefits, and the surviving spouse's earnings.

Net Annual Income Needed
Present income, less the spending no longer required, and less the income available, determines the income needs for the survivors to sustain their current standard of living.

Insurance Required to Provide Needed Income

To estimate the required amount of insurance, multiply the income required by 12.5. This assumes the survivors will earn an 8% return, after taxes, on the insurance proceeds.

> Example: $10,000 additional annual income is needed to support the survivors.
> $10,000 x 12.5 = $125,000 in insurance invested at 8% would provide the needed income.

Lump Sum Requirements

In addition to insurance required to produce income, lump sums may be required for specific purposes or debt repayment. Those needs should be determined and added to the total amount of the insurance.

THE FILING SYSTEM

It is important to keep invoices, checks and receipts that are necessary for your income tax records, or are the only evidence of a paid bill. We suggest that you file them in a shoe box or in a box of similar size, using a separate box for each year. Simple dividers are adequate with the following suggested headings: Income, Tithe/Giving, Medical, Business Expenses, Insurance, Interest, Taxes, Automobile, Utilities, Telephone, Home Improvements, Credit Card Statements, and Bank Statements.

   You may add or delete categories depending upon your personal needs. After the year ends, label the receipts for each category and secure them with a rubber band. You may then remove the dividers and use them the following year.

Bill Organizer

For many of us, it is a challenge to keep track of our bills. We developed the *Bill Organizer*™ to help you do just that. The *Bill Organizer*™ is an expanding file containing 12 tabbed pockets that can be customized to organize your bills by either category or due date.

Life Insurance Worksheet

GROSS MONTHLY INCOME

Present annual income needs:	53,200
Subtract deceased person's needs:	9,000
Subtract other income available: (Social Security, investments, retirement)	10,000
= Net annual income needed:	34,200

Net annual income needed, multiplied by 12.5 (assumes an 8% after-tax investment return on insurance proceeds): 427,500

Lump sum needs:

Debts:	8,000
Education:	20,000
Other:	0
Total lump sum needs:	28,000

Total Life Insurance Needs: 455,500

Don and Janet's Life Insurance Worksheet

GROSS MONTHLY INCOME

Present annual income needs:	_____
Subtract deceased person's needs:	_____
Subtract other income available: (Social Security, investments, retirement)	_____
= Net annual income needed:	_____

Net annual income needed, multiplied by 12.5 (assumes an 8% after-tax investment return on insurance proceeds):

Lump sum needs:

Debts:	_____
Education:	_____
Other:	_____
Total lump sum needs:	

Total Life Insurance Needs:

Once you have quantified your approximate life insurance needs, deduct the amount of your present life insurance coverage to determine whether you need additional life insurance. Then analyze your budget to determine how much new insurance you can afford. Seek counsel to decide the precise amount and type of insurance that would meet your needs and budget.

The Children Notes end with this statement: "I have yet to meet an adult whose parents lived these biblical financial principles and taught them systematically to their children." As an unfortunate consequence, children leave home ill-equipped to manage their financial future. I pray our generation will be more faithful in this area.

This week's practical application starting on page 100 is designed as a checklist to help you to train children to earn and maintain money from a biblical perspective. We recommend that you review this once each year to evaluate your progress in training children.

Helping Children Apply God's Financial Principles

This Bible study is full of activities to help make learning fun and exciting. Designed for ages 7 and younger.

The ABC's of Handling Money God's Way — #AB2008

Leader's Guide — #AL2009

Four children with a financial challenge learn the secret of giving, saving, spending, and much more. They also discover that they can trust God to provide. The principles are embedded in a story of adventure that captures and holds the attention of children ages 8-12.

The Secret — #SC2005

Leader's Guide — #SL2006

They've just received their allowances. What will your kids do with the money? The first player to meet his or her giving, saving, and spending goals wins the game! Designed for ages 5-10.

Money Matters for Kids™ board game — #KG930

My Giving Bank has been designed to teach your child the value of money and how to handle it in a way that is pleasing to God. When you order this 3-compartment bank of transparent plastic from Crown, we also include a supplementary audio cassette and pamphlet. Designed for ages 3 and up.

My Giving Bank — #PK004

For more information, call 1-800-722-1976 or visit us at www.crown.org.

Organizing Your Children

Date: __January 1__

LEARNING MONEY MANAGEMENT

INCOME

Are your children receiving an income? __Yes__

Are they performing routine chores around the house in return for their income? __Yes__

Describe what they must purchase with their income: __John must buy school supplies. Ruth buys her gum.__

BUDGETING

Are your children budgeting? __Yes__

Describe the method they are using to budget: __Both are using the Giving–Saving–Spending bank.__

If your children are involved in the family budget, describe their participation: __John is beginning to participate in our budget discussions. Ruth is too young.__

SAVING AND INVESTMENTS

Is there a savings account opened in the name of your child? __Yes__

Have you taught your child the concept of compound interest? __No__

Describe the level of your child's understanding of how standard investments function (i.e., the stock market, bonds, real estate, insurance): __They both understand the banks pay them interest on their savings.__

DEBT

Have you taught your children the principles of debt? __Yes__

Are they aware of the true cost of interest? __No__

GIVING

Have you taught your children the principles of giving? __Yes__

Describe their giving? __John gives $1 and Ruth gives 25¢ each week to church.__

Organizing Your Children

ROUTINE RESPONSIBILITIES

Describe the routine unpaid chores each child is required to perform: __Both clean their rooms and empty garbage.__

How do you hold them accountable to be faithful with their chores? __We do not, but will begin to use a list of chores and check them when done.__

EXPOSING YOUR CHILDREN TO YOUR WORK

Have you exposed your children to your means of making a living? __Yes__

How would your children describe your job? __Daddy helps people get insurance.__

Describe any way your children could participate in working with you: __They are not yet old enough to help.__

EARNING EXTRA MONEY

Do your children have the opportunity to earn extra money working around the house? __Yes__

If so, describe these money making opportunities: __John mows the lawn and washes the car. Ruth cleans the inside of the car.__

WORKING FOR OTHERS

Describe the jobs your children perform for others: __John mows the neighbor's lawn and washes the car. Ruth is too young.__

STRATEGY FOR INDEPENDENCE

Describe the strategy you will use to prepare your children to independently earn and manage their money by the time they leave your home: __We will slowly increase their responsibilities for money management and money making until they become responsible for all their needs with the exception of food by their last year of high school.__

ORGANIZING YOUR CHILDREN

Organizing Your Children

Date: _____

LEARNING MONEY MANAGEMENT

INCOME

Are your children receiving an income? _____

Are they performing routine chores around the house in return for their income? _____

Describe what they must purchase with their income: _____

_____

_____

BUDGETING

Are your children budgeting? _____

Describe the method they are using to budget: _____

_____

If your children are involved in the family budget, describe their participation:

_____

_____

SAVING AND INVESTMENTS

Is there a savings account opened in the name of your child? _____

Have you taught your child the concept of compound interest? _____

Describe the level of your child's understanding of how standard investments function
(i.e., the stock market, bonds, real estate, insurance): _____

_____

_____

DEBT

Have you taught your children the principles of debt? _____

Are they aware of the true cost of interest? _____

GIVING

Have you taught your children the principles of giving? _____

Describe their giving? _____

Organizing Your Children

ROUTINE RESPONSIBILITIES

Describe the routine unpaid chores each child is required to perform: _____

_____

How do you hold them accountable to be faithful with their chores? _____

_____

_____

EXPOSING YOUR CHILDREN TO YOUR WORK

Have you exposed your children to your means of making a living? _____

How would your children describe your job? _____

_____

_____

Describe any way your children could participate in working with you: _____

_____

_____

EARNING EXTRA MONEY

Do your children have the opportunity to earn extra money working around the house?

_____

If so, describe these money making opportunities: _____

_____

_____

WORKING FOR OTHERS

Describe the jobs your children perform for others: _____

_____

_____

STRATEGY FOR INDEPENDENCE

Describe the strategy you will use to prepare your children to independently earn and manage their money by the time they leave your home: _____

_____

_____

_____

DETERMINING YOUR STANDARD OF LIVING

The Bible does not prescribe one standard of living for everyone. Each individual's standard of living should be prayerfully determined. Write down a description of what you (and your spouse, if you are married) determine is your God-given standard of living after you read the Perspective Notes and review your financial goals on pages 20 and 21 of this workbook.

Don and Janet's standard of living:

We would be satisfied living in our present home (not moving to a larger or more expensive home). We have the goal of adding a porch on our home. We want to concentrate on educating our children, paying off our debts, giving more and saving, rather than increasing our standard of living for the next fifteen years. After we have accomplished our financial goals, we want to travel once a year and give one-third of our income. We would like to keep our cars an average of seven years and purchase low-mileage used cars. We want to maintain a simple and more "classic" wardrobe rather than following the latest clothing fads. We also want to help our children purchase their first home. We want everything we spend to please the Lord.

Your standard of living:

CONTROL IMPULSE SPENDING

This is the biggest budget buster for many of us. I have a friend who controls impulse spending by using an "impulse list." If he wants to buy anything that is not contemplated in his budget, he writes the item on his impulse list and then prays about the item for two weeks. Rarely does he buy anything on the list, because impulses usually pass. If a quick decision is required, be cautious. Take the time to think and pray.

THINK YEARLY

We have been conditioned to think of our spending on a monthly, weekly or even daily basis. When we analyze an expense on an annual basis, it gives us a much better perspective of the cost. If you eat lunch out every working day and spend an average of $4 for each meal, it does not seem like much money. But this equals $1,000 a year. Even a daily newspaper can add up to more than $200 a year. There are many creative ways we can reduce these expenses once we recognize their true impact on our budget. For instance, if I have a close neighbor, we can share the newspaper and save half the cost. As we analyze our spending on a yearly basis, it will become apparent that the small "nickel and dime" expenditures have a significant impact on the budget.

FOOD

- Prepare a menu for the week and shop only for the ingredients you are going to need for the menu.

- Never shop when hungry. I am "a disaster waiting to happen" when I'm hungry in the grocery store!

- If possible, brown bag your lunch at work. This is an effective way of saving on the lunch purchase and controlling your weight as well.

- Review your household eating and drinking habits. Junk food and soft drinks are expensive and damaging to your health. Never buy them.

- A Department of Agriculture study found it costs approximately 80% more to have a comparable meal at a fast-food restaurant than at home. When eating out, drink water for your beverage and have dessert at home.

TRANSPORTATION

Reduce the use of your automobile. Drive efficiently by doing your errands in as few trips as possible. Walk, bike more, or use mass transit if it is available. A rent-a-car study found ownership and operating costs for a typical new compact car driven 10,000 miles per year for five years were 47 cents a mile. The less you drive, the less you spend.

STANDARD OF LIVING & WISE SPENDING

CLOTHING

- Select one or two basic colors for your wardrobe. My mother says she can tell my brother and me apart because he always wears brown and I am always in blue. You can save money by purchasing traditional fashions in basic colors.

- Swap children's clothes with friends and relatives.

RECREATION

- Cultivate inexpensive hobbies and pleasures: books from the library and scenic walks. Try not to confuse shopping with fun.

- All pets cost money. Limit pets to those you really enjoy and can afford.

- Plan vacations during the "off seasons" if possible. Consider a camping vacation to avoid motel and food expenses. Select vacation locations in your general area.

HEALTH

Practice preventive medicine. Your body will stay healthier when you get the proper amounts of sleep, exercise and nutrition. Also practice proper oral hygiene for proper teeth – and for a reduction in dental bills!

HOUSING

- Give your home a thorough energy check for proper insulation and caulking. Federal law requires all utility companies to offer a free energy audit of your home. Many utility companies publish booklets with excellent energy-saving ideas.

- When placing long distance phone calls, call during the periods of lowest rates.

- Secure several written bids for work that needs to be done. There can be a substantial cost differential among bidders.

INVOLVEMENT AND SUGGESTIONS

Please Print   Date:_____

YOUR NAME   ☐ MR   ☐ MRS   ☐ MISS   ☐ DR   ☐ REV

HOME ADDRESS

CITY   ST/PROV   ZIP/POSTAL CODE

COUNTRY

HOME PHONE   WORK PHONE

CHURCH   CITY   ST/PROV

E-MAIL ADDRESS

We want to seek your counsel. The suggestions and insights of past students have significantly improved the study. We also want to invite you to join with us in helping to train others to handle money biblically. Please complete this and send it to CROWN FINANCIAL MINISTRIES, PO Box 100, Gainesville GA 30503-0100. If more convenient, you may visit our Web site **www.crown.org/isform.asp** and complete this form electronically. As a special thank-you for completing this form, we will send you a free CROWN lapel pin!

INVOLVEMENT

PRAY

☐ Yes, I would like to pray regularly for the Lord to expand CROWN and change lives through this ministry.

SERVE

Please send me information on:

☐ Becoming trained as a small group leader.
☐ Becoming trained as a budget counselor.
☐ Hosting a CROWN financial seminar in my church or town.

SUPPORT

☐ Enclosed is a contribution to CROWN in the amount of $_____.
☐ Please send information on how to become a regular supporter of CROWN (Outreach Partner).

NEWSLETTER AND E-MAIL

We send a weekly e-mail message and monthly newsletter sharing God's principles and communicating what the Lord is doing in CROWN FINANCIAL MINISTRIES. Please indicate below if you would like to receive these.

☐ Yes, I would like to like to receive the weekly e-mail message.
☐ Yes, I would like to receive the monthly *Money Matters* newsletter.

1. What was the most valuable part of the study? Please be specific.

2. Do you have any suggestions for improving any areas?

3. Describe any insights that would help others.

We would be very appreciative if you would share what the Lord has done in your life through this study, or if you have any practical hints that would be especially helpful for other people.

Discovering God's Way of Handling Money

VIDEO SERIES

Designed to be used either for individual study or in a Sunday school setting or weekend seminar, this eight-week video series will have a profound impact on the adults in your church. Learning how to correctly manage your money will affect your relationship with God.

Discovering God's Way of Handling Money is a two-volume video series with a course workbook for each student. A leader's guide is also available to give you everything you need to guide students through the series. Each video contains four sessions that cover such topics as debt, honesty, giving, work, saving and investing, and more!

Discovering God's Way of Handling Money **Video Series** . . . . #DV4002 $35.00
(2-video set, 4 sessions per video)   Publisher's retail price: $35.00

Discovering God's Way of Handling Money **Course Workbook** . . . . . . #DW2003 $8.00
(80 pages, softcover)   Publisher's retail price: $8.00

Discovering God's Way of Handling Money **Leader's Guide** . . . . #DL2004 $8.00
(80 pages, softcover)   Publisher's retail price: $8.00

Please note: Prices are subject to change at any time, while supplies last. To check latest prices, call or visit our Web site.

Newsletter

CROWN FINANCIAL MINISTRIES' monthly *Money Matters* newsletter communicates our perspective on economic events and provides timely articles and news that can be applied in everyday life. It is designed to help you become a more effective steward of the resources God has entrusted to you.

When you order CROWN FINANCIAL MINISTRIES materials, you are automatically placed on our newsletter mailing list. If you do not wish to order materials but would like to receive the newsletter, please contact us. There is no charge to receive *Money Matters* newsletter; however, contributions are welcome. Call us at 770-534-1000 for more information.